THE TENTH AMENDMENT

The ★★★★★★★ AMERICAN HERITAGE HISTORY *of the* BILL *of* RIGHTS

THE TENTH AMENDMENT

Judith Adams

Introduction by
WARREN E. BURGER
Chief Justice of the United States
1969–1986

Silver Burdett Press

This book is dedicated to a very special person, Paul, with love.

Cover: State flags at the Lincoln Memorial, Washington, D.C. According to the Tenth Amendment, the powers not delegated to the United States by the Constitution, nor prohibited by it to the states, are reserved to the states or to the people.

CONSULTANTS:

Charles A. Lofgren
Professor of American
  Politics and History
Claremont McKenna College
Claremont, California

Michael H. Reggio
Law-Related Education
  Coordinator
Oklahoma Bar Association
Oklahoma City, Oklahoma

Frank de Varona
Associate Superintendant
Dade County Public Schools
Miami, Florida

Text and Cover Design: Circa 86, Inc.

Library of Congress Cataloging-in-Publication Data

Adams, Judith
   The Tenth Amendment/by Judith Adams: with an introduction
by Warren E. Burger.
   p. cm.—(The American Heritage history of the Bill of
Rights)
   Includes indexes.
   Includes bibliographical references.
   Summary: Examines the provisions of the Tenth Amendment, which speaks of the powers of the Federal government in relation to the powers of individual states and the people.
   1. United States—Constitutional law—Amendments—10th—History—
Juvenile literature. 2. Federal government—United States—
History—Juvenile literature. 3. State rights—History—Juvenile
literature. [1. United States—Constitutional law—
Amendments—10th—History. 2. Federal government—History.
3. State rights—History.] I. Title. II. Series.
KF4558 10th.A33 1991
342.73'042—dc20
[347.30242]
                                                        90-20069
                                                             CIP
                                                              AC

Manufactured in the United States of America.

ISBN 0-382-24189-4 [lib. bdg.]
10 9 8 7 6 5 4 3 2 1

ISBN 0-382-24201-7 [pbk.]
10 9 8 7 6 5 4 3 2 1

$\mathscr{C}$ONTENTS

INTRODUCTION

WARREN E. BURGER
Chief Justice of the United States, 1969–1986

The Tenth Amendment embodies the skepticism, even fear, of many of the Framers of the Constitution regarding a strong federal government. It reserves to the states, or to the people themselves, any powers neither delegated to the federal government nor specifically prohibited to the states by the Constitution. It is a strong statement in favor of individual liberty—one of the strongest in the Bill of Rights. Two hundred years ago people were worried about the new "monster" national government they were creating.

Concepts of liberty—the values liberty protects—inspired the Framers of our Constitution and the Bill of Rights to some of their most impassioned eloquence. "Liberty, the greatest of earthly possessions—give us that precious jewel, and you may take everything else," declaimed Patrick Henry. Those toilers in the "vineyard of liberty" sensed the historic nature of their mission, and their foresight accounts for the survival of the Bill of Rights.

It took the cataclysm of the Civil War to settle the issue of the primacy of the federal government in domestic affairs. Following the war, the federal government, through acts of Congress, executive actions, and decisions by the Supreme Court, expanded its power, authority, and influence within the states. This power was manifested in the role of the federal government during Reconstruction, later in the New Deal, and more recently in civil rights enforcement. In recent years, courts and successive administrations have sought a realignment of federal and state responsibilities, under such terms as "creative federalism" or "new federalism." Such initiatives demonstrate that the idea of divided powers expressed in the Tenth Amendment still influences our system of government.

The long-term success of the system of ordered liberty set up by our Constitution was by no means foreordained. The bicentennial of the Bill of Rights provides an opportunity to reflect on the significance of the freedoms we enjoy and to commit ourselves to exercise the civic responsibilities required to sustain our constitutional system. The

Constitution, including its first ten amendments, the Bill of Rights, has survived two centuries because of its unprecedented philosophical premise: that it derives its power from the people. It is not a grant from the government to the people. In 1787 the masters—the people—were saying to their government—their servant—that certain rights are inherent, natural rights and that they belong to the people, who had those rights before any governments existed. The function of government, they said, was to protect these rights.

The Bill of Rights also owes its continued vitality to the fact that it was drafted by experienced, practical politicians. It was a product of the Framers' essential mistrust of the frailties of human nature. This led them to develop the idea of the separation of powers and to make the Bill of Rights part of the permanent Constitution.

Moreover, the document was designed to be flexible, and the role of providing that flexibility through interpretation has fallen to the judiciary. Indeed, the first commander in chief, George Washington, gave the Supreme Court its moral marching orders two centuries ago when he said, "the administration of justice is the firmest pillar of government." The principle of judicial review as a check on government has perhaps nowhere been more significant than in the protection of individual liberties. It has been my privilege, along with my colleagues on the Court, to ensure the continued vitality of our Bill of Rights. As John Marshall asked, long before he became chief justice, "To what quarter will you look for a protection from an infringement on the Constitution, if you will not give the power to the judiciary?"

But the preservation of the Bill of Rights is not the sole responsibility of the judiciary. Rather, judges, legislatures, and presidents are partners with every American; liberty is the responsibility of every public officer and every citizen. In this spirit all Americans should become acquainted with the principles and history of this most remarkable document. Its bicentennial should not be simply a celebration but the beginning of an ongoing process. Americans must—by their conduct—guarantee that it continues to protect the sacred rights of our uniquely multicultural population. We must not fail to exercise our rights to vote, to participate in government and community activities, and to implement the principles of liberty, tolerance, opportunity, and justice for all.

THE AMERICAN HERITAGE
HISTORY OF THE BILL OF RIGHTS

The Bill of Rights

AMENDMENT 1*
Article Congress shall make no law respecting an establishment of religion, or prohibiting the free exercise thereof; or abridging the freedom of speech, or of the press; or the right of the people peaceably to assemble, and to petition the Government for a redress of grievances.

AMENDMENT 2
Article A well regulated Militia, being necessary to the security of a free State, the right of the people to keep and bear Arms, shall not be infringed.

AMENDMENT 3
Article No Soldier shall, in time of peace be quartered in any house, without the consent of the Owner, nor in time of war, but in a manner to be prescribed by law.

AMENDMENT 4
Article The right of the people to be secure in their persons, houses, papers, and effects, against unreasonable searches and seizures, shall not be violated, and no Warrants shall issue, but upon probable cause, supported by Oath or affirmation, and particularly describing the place to be searched, and the persons or things to be seized.

AMENDMENT 5
Article No person shall be held to answer for a capital, or otherwise infamous crime, unless on a presentment or indictment of a Grand Jury, except in cases arising in the land or naval forces, or in the Militia, when in actual service in time of War or public danger; nor shall any person be subject for the same offence to be twice put in jeopardy of life or limb; nor shall be compelled in any criminal case to be a witness against himself, nor be deprived of life, liberty, or property, without due process of law; nor shall private property be taken for public use without just compensation.

AMENDMENT 6
Article In all criminal prosecutions, the accused shall enjoy the right to a speedy and public trial, by an impartial jury of the State and district wherein the crime shall have been committed, which district shall have been previously ascertained by law, and to be informed of the nature and cause of the accusation; to be confronted with the witnesses against him; to have compulsory process for obtaining Witnesses in his favor, and to have the assistance of counsel for his defence.

AMENDMENT 7
Article In Suits at common law, where the value in controversy shall exceed twenty dollars, the right of trial by jury shall be preserved, and no fact tried by a jury, shall be otherwise reexamined in any Court of the United States, than according to the rules of the common law.

AMENDMENT 8
Article Excessive bail shall not be required, nor excessive fines imposed, nor cruel and unusual punishments inflicted.

AMENDMENT 9
Article The enumeration in the Constitution, of certain rights, shall not be construed to deny or disparage others retained by the people.

AMENDMENT 10
Article The powers not delegated to the United States by the Constitution, nor prohibited by it to the States, are reserved to the States respectively, or to the people.

*Note that each of the first ten amendments to the original Constitution is called an "Article." None of these amendments had actual numbers at the time of their ratification.

TIME CHART

THE HISTORY OF THE
BILL OF RIGHTS

1770s–1790s

1774	Quartering Act
1775	Revolutionary War begins
1776	Declaration of Independence is signed.
1783	Revolutionary War ends.
1787	Constitutional Convention writes the U.S. Constitution.
1788	U.S. Constitution is ratified by most states.
1789	Congress proposes the Bill of Rights
1791	The Bill of Rights is ratified by the states.
1792	Militia Act

1800s–1820s

1803	*Marbury* v. *Madison.* Supreme Court declares that it has the power of judicial review and exercises it. This is the first case in which the Court holds a law of Congress unconstitutional.
1807	Trial of Aaron Burr. Ruling that juries may have knowledge of a case so long as they have not yet formed an opinion.
1813	Kentucky becomes the first state to outlaw concealed weapons.
1824	*Gibbons* v. *Ogden.* Supreme Court defines Congress's power to regulate commerce, including trade between states and within states if that commerce affects other states.

1830s–1870s

1833 *Barron* v. *Baltimore.* Supreme Court rules that Bill of Rights applies only to actions of the federal government, not to the states and local governments.

1851 *Cooley* v. *Board of Wardens of the Port of Philadelphia.* Supreme Court rules that states can apply their own rules to some foreign and interstate commerce if their rules are of a local nature—unless or until Congress makes rules for particular situations.

1857 *Dred Scott* v. *Sandford.* Supreme Court denies that African Americans are citizens even if they happen to live in a "free state."

1862 Militia Act

1865 Thirteenth Amendment is ratified. Slavery is not allowed in the United States.

1868 Fourteenth Amendment is ratified. All people born or naturalized in the United States are citizens. Their privileges and immunities are protected, as are their life, liberty, and property according to due process. They have equal protection of the laws.

1873 *Slaughterhouse* cases. Supreme Court rules that the Fourteenth Amendment does not limit state power to make laws dealing with economic matters. Court mentions the unenumerated right to political participation.

1876 *United States* v. *Cruikshank.* Supreme Court rules that the right to bear arms for a lawful purpose is not an absolute right granted by the Constitution. States can limit this right and make their own gun-control laws.

1880s–1920s

1884 *Hurtado* v. *California.* Supreme Court rules that the right to a grand jury indictment doesn't apply to the states.

1896 *Plessy* v. *Ferguson.* Supreme Court upholds a state law based on "separate but equal" facilities for different races.

1903 Militia Act creates National Guard.

1905 *Lochner* v. *New York.* Supreme Court strikes down a state law regulating maximum work hours.

1914 *Weeks* v. *United States.* Supreme Court establishes that illegally obtained evidence, obtained by unreasonable search and seizure, cannot be used in federal trials.

1918 *Hammer* v. *Dagenhart.* Supreme Court declares unconstitutional a federal law prohibiting the shipment between states of goods made by young children.

1923 *Meyer* v. *Nebraska.* Supreme Court rules that a law banning teaching of foreign languages or teaching in languages other than English is unconstitutional. Court says that certain areas of people's private lives are protected from government interference.

1925 *Carroll* v. *United States.* Supreme Court allows searches of automobiles without a search warrant under some circumstances.

1925 *Gitlow* v. *New York.* Supreme Court rules that freedom of speech and freedom of the press are protected from state actions by the Fourteenth Amendment.

1930s

1931 *Near* v. *Minnesota*. Supreme Court rules that liberty of the press and of speech are safe-guarded from state action.

1931 *Stromberg* v. *California*. Supreme Court extends concept of freedom of speech to symbolic actions such as displaying a flag.

1932 *Powell* v. *Alabama* (*First Scottsboro* case). Supreme Court rules that poor defendants have a right to an appointed lawyer when tried for crimes that may result in the death penalty.

1934 National Firearms Act becomes the first federal law to restrict the keeping and bearing of arms.

1935 *Norris* v. *Alabama* (*Second Scottsboro* case). Supreme Court reverses the conviction of an African American because of the long continued excluding of African Americans from jury service in the trial area.

1937 *Palko* v. *Connecticut*. Supreme Court refuses to require states to protect people under the double jeopardy clause of the Bill of Rights. But the case leads to future application of individual rights in the Bill of Rights to the states on a case-by-case basis.

1937 *DeJonge* v. *Oregon*. Supreme Court rules that freedom of assembly and petition are protected against state laws.

1939 *United States* v. *Miller*. Supreme Court rules that National Firearms Act of 1934 does not violate Second Amendment.

1940s–1950s

1940 *Cantwell* v. *Connecticut*. Supreme Court rules that free exercise of religion is protected against state laws.

1943 *Barnette* v. *West Virginia State Board of Education*. Supreme Court rules that flag salute laws are unconstitutional.

1946 *Theil* v. *Pacific Railroad*. Juries must be a cross section of the community, excluding no group based on religion, race, sex, or economic status.

1947 *Everson* v. *Board of Education*. Supreme Court rules that government attempts to impose religious practices, the establishment of religion, is forbidden to the states.

1948 *In re Oliver*. Supreme Court rules that defendants have a right to public trial in nonfederal trials.

1949 *Wolf* v. *California*. Supreme Court rules that freedom from unreasonable searches and seizures also applies to states.

1954 *Brown* v. *Board of Education of Topeka*. Supreme Court holds that segregation on the basis of race (in public education) denies equal protection of the laws.

1958 *NAACP* v. *Alabama*. Supreme Court rules that the privacy of membership lists in an organization is part of the right to freedom of assembly and association.

1960s

1961 *Mapp* v. *Ohio*. Supreme Court rules that illegally obtained evidence must not be allowed in state criminal trials.

1962 *Engel* v. *Vitale*. Supreme Court strikes down state-sponsored school prayer, saying it is no business of government to compose official prayers as part of a religious program carried on by the government.

1963 *Gideon* v. *Wainwright*. Supreme Court rules that the right of people accused of serious crimes to be represented by an appointed counsel applies to state criminal trials.

1964 Civil Rights Act is passed.

1964 *Malloy* v. *Hogan*. Supreme Court rules that the right to protection against forced self-incrimination applies to state trials.

1965 *Griswold* v. *Connecticut*. Supreme Court rules that there is a right to privacy in marriage and declares unconstitutional a state law banning the use of or the giving of information about birth control.

1965 *Pointer* v. *Texas*. Supreme Court rules that the right to confront witnesses against an accused person applies to state trials.

1966 *Parker* v. *Gladden*. Supreme Court ruling is interpreted to mean that the right to an impartial jury is applied to the states.

1966 *Miranda* v. *Arizona*. Supreme Court extends the protection against forced self-incrimination. Police have to inform people in custody of their rights before questioning them.

1967 *Katz* v. *United States*. Supreme Court rules that people's right to be free of unreasonable searches includes protection against electronic surveillance.

1967 *Washington* v. *Texas*. Supreme Court rules that accused people have the right to have witnesses in their favor brought into court.

1967 *In re Gault*. Supreme Court rules that juvenile proceedings that might lead to the young person's being sent to a state institution must follow due process and fair treatment. These include the rights against forced self-incrimination, to counsel, to confront witnesses.

1967 *Klopfer* v. *North Carolina*. Supreme Court rules that the right to a speedy trial applies to state trials.

1968 *Duncan* v. *Louisiana*. Supreme Court rules that the right to a jury trial in criminal cases applies to state trials.

1969 *Benton* v. *Maryland*. Supreme Court rules that the protection against double jeopardy applies to the states.

1969 *Brandenburg* v. *Ohio*. Supreme Court rules that speech calling for the use of force or crime can only be prohibited if it is directed to bringing about immediate lawless action and is likely to bring about such action.

1970s–1990s

1970 *Williams* v. *Florida*. Juries in cases that do not lead to the possibility of the death penalty may consist of six jurors rather than twelve.

1971 *Pentagon Papers* case. Freedom of the press is protected by forbidding prior restraint.

1971 *Duke Power Co.* v. *Carolina Environmental Study Group, Inc.* Supreme Court upholds state law limiting liability of federally licensed power companies in the event of a nuclear accident.

1972 *Furman* v. *Georgia*. Supreme Court rules that the death penalty (as it was then decided upon) is cruel and unusual punishment and therefore unconstitutional.

1972 *Argersinger* v. *Hamlin*. Supreme Court rules that right to counsel applies to all criminal cases that might involve a jail term.

1973 *Roe* v. *Wade*. Supreme Court declares that the right to privacy protects a woman's right to end pregnancy by abortion under specified circumstances.

1976 *Gregg* v. *Georgia*. Supreme Court rules that the death penalty is to be allowed if it is decided upon in a consistent and reasonable way, if the sentencing follows strict guidelines, and if the penalty is not required for certain crimes.

1976 *National League of Cities* v. *Usery*. Supreme Court holds that the Tenth Amendment prevents Congress from making federal minimum wage and overtime rules apply to state and city workers.

1981 *Quilici* v. *Village of Morton Grove*. U.S. district court upholds a local ban on sale and possession of handguns.

1985 *Garcia* v. *San Antonio Metropolitan Transit Authority*. Supreme Court rules that Congress can make laws dealing with wages and hour rules applied to city-owned transportation systems.

1989 *Webster* v. *Reproductive Health Services*. Supreme Court holds that a state may prohibit all use of public facilities and publicly employed staff in abortions.

1989 *Johnson* v. *Texas*. Supreme Court rules that flag burning is protected and is a form of "symbolic speech."

1990 *Cruzan* v. *Missouri Department of Health*. Supreme Court recognizes for the first time a very sick person's right to die without being forced to undergo unwanted medical treatment and a person's right to a living will.

1990 *Noriega–CNN* case. Supreme Court upholds lower federal court's decision to allow temporary prior restraint thus limiting the First Amendment right of freedom of the press.

The Birth of the Bill of Rights

"We hold these truths to be self-evident, that all men are created equal,
that they are endowed by their Creator with certain unalienable Rights,
that among these are Life, Liberty, and the pursuit of Happiness."

THE DECLARATION OF INDEPENDENCE (1776)

A brave Chinese student standing in front of a line of tanks,
Eastern Europeans marching against the secret police, happy
crowds dancing on top of the Berlin Wall—these were recent scenes
of people trying to gain their freedom or celebrating it. The scenes
and the events that sparked them will live on in history. They also
show the lasting gift that is our Bill of Rights. The freedoms
guaranteed by the Bill of Rights have guided and inspired millions
of people all over the world in their struggle for freedom.

The Colonies Gain Their Freedom

Like many countries today, the United States fought to gain
freedom and democracy for itself. The American colonies had a
revolution from 1775 to 1783 to free themselves from British rule.

The colonists fought to free themselves because they believed
that the British had violated, or gone against, their rights. The
colonists held what some considered the extreme idea that all

James Madison is known as both the "Father of the Constitution" and the
"Father of the Bill of Rights." In 1789 he proposed to Congress the
amendments that became the Bill of Rights. Madison served two terms as
president of the United States from 1809 to 1817.

15

The Raising of the Liberty Pole by John McRae. In 1776, American colonists hoisted liberty poles as symbols of liberty and freedom from British rule. At the top they usually placed a liberty cap. Such caps resembled the caps given to slaves in ancient Rome when they were freed.

persons are born with certain rights. They believed that these rights could not be taken away, even by the government. The importance our nation gave to individual rights can be seen in the Declaration of Independence. The Declaration, written by Thomas Jefferson in 1776, states:

> We hold these truths to be self-evident, that all men are created equal, that they are endowed by their Creator with certain unalienable Rights, that among these are Life, Liberty, and the pursuit of Happiness.

The United States won its independence from Britain in 1783. But with freedom came the difficult job of forming a government. The Americans wanted a government that was strong enough to keep peace and prosperity, but not so strong that it might take away the rights for which the Revolution had been fought. The Articles of Confederation was the country's first written plan of government.

The Articles of Confederation, becoming law in 1781, created a weak national government. The defects in the Articles soon became clear to many Americans. Because the United States did not have a strong national government, its economy suffered. Under the Articles, Congress did not have the power to tax. It had to ask the states for money or borrow it. There was no separate president or court system. Nine of the states had to agree before Congress's bills became law. In 1786 economic problems caused farmers in Massachusetts to revolt. The national government was almost powerless to stop the revolt. It was also unable to build an army or navy strong enough to protect the United States's borders and its ships on the high seas.

The Constitution Is Drawn Up

The nation's problems had to be solved. So, in February 1787, the Continental Congress asked the states to send delegates to a convention to discuss ways of improving the Articles. That May, fifty-five delegates, from every state except Rhode Island, met in Philadelphia. The group included some of the country's most famous leaders: George Washington, hero of the Revolution; Benjamin Franklin, publisher, inventor, and diplomat; and James Madison, a leading critic of the Articles. Madison would soon become the guiding force behind the Constitutional Convention.

After a long, hot summer of debate the delegates finally drew up the document that became the U.S. Constitution. It set up a strong central government. But it also divided power between three branches of the federal government. These three branches were the executive branch (the presidency), the legislative branch (Congress), and the judicial branch (the courts). Each was given one part of the government's power. This division was to make sure that no single branch became so powerful that it could violate the people's rights.

The legislative branch (made up of the House of Representatives and the Senate) would have the power to pass laws, raise taxes and spend money, regulate the national economy, and declare war. The executive branch was given the power to carry out the laws, run foreign affairs, and command the military.

The Signing of the Constitution painted by Thomas Rossiter. The Constitutional Convention met in Philadelphia from May into September 1787. The proposed Constitution contained protection for some individual rights such as protection against *ex post facto* laws and bills of attainder. When the Constitution was ratified by the required number of states in 1788, however, it did not have a bill of rights.

The role of the judicial branch in this plan was less clear. The Constitution said that the judicial branch would have "judicial power." However, it was unclear exactly what this power was. Over the years "judicial power" has come to mean "judicial review." The power of judicial review allows the federal courts to reject laws passed by Congress or the state legislatures that they believe violate the Constitution.

Judicial review helps protect our rights. It allows federal courts to reject laws that violate the Constitution's guarantees of individual rights. Because of this power, James Madison believed that the courts would be an "impenetrable bulwark," an unbreakable wall, against any attempt by government to take away these rights.

The Constitution did more than divide the power of the federal government among the three branches. It also divided power between the states and the federal government. This division of power is known as *federalism*. Federalism means that the federal

government has control over certain areas. These include regulating the national economy and running foreign and military affairs. The states have control over most other areas. For example, they regulate their economies and make most other laws. Once again, the Framers (writers) of the Constitution hoped that the division of powers would keep both the states and the federal government from becoming too strong and possibly violating individual rights.

The new Constitution did *not,* however, contain a bill of rights. Such a bill would list the people's rights and would forbid the government from interfering with them. The only discussion of the topic came late in the convention. At that time, George Mason of Virginia called for a bill of rights. A Connecticut delegate, Roger Sherman, disagreed. He claimed that a bill of rights was not needed. In his view, the Constitution did not take away any of the rights in the bills of rights in the state constitutions. These had been put in place during the Revolution. The other delegates agreed with Roger Sherman. Mason's proposal was voted down by all.

Yet the Constitution was not without guarantees of individual rights. One of these rights was the protection of *habeas corpus.* This is a legal term that refers to the right of someone who has been arrested to be brought into court and formally charged with a crime. Another right forbade *ex post facto* laws. These are laws that outlaw actions that took place before the passage of the laws. Other parts of the Constitution forbade bills of attainder (laws pronouncing a person guilty of a crime without trial), required jury trials, restricted convictions for treason, and guaranteed a republican form of government. That is a government in which political power rests with citizens who vote for elected officials and representatives responsible to the voters. The Constitution also forbade making public officials pass any "religious test." This meant that religious requirements could not be forced on public officials.

The Debate Over the New Constitution

Once it was written, the Constitution had to be ratified, or approved, by nine of the states before it could go into effect. The new

Constitution created much controversy. Heated battles raged in many states over whether or not to approve the document. One of the main arguments used by those who opposed the Constitution (the Anti-Federalists) was that the Constitution made the federal government too strong. They feared that it might violate the rights of the people just as the British government had. Although he had helped write the Constitution, Anti-Federalist George Mason opposed it for this reason. He claimed that he would sooner chop off his right hand than put it to the Constitution as it then stood.

To correct what they viewed as flaws in the Constitution, the Anti-Federalists insisted that it have a bill of rights. The fiery orator of the Revolution, Patrick Henry, another Anti-Federalist, exclaimed, "Liberty, the greatest of all earthly blessings—give us that precious jewel, and you may take every thing else!"

Although he was not an Anti-Federalist, Thomas Jefferson also believed that a bill of rights was needed. He wrote a letter to James Madison, a wavering Federalist, in which he said: "A bill of rights is what the people are entitled to against every government on earth."

Supporters of the Constitution (the Federalists) argued that it did not need a bill of rights. One reason they stated, similar to that given at the Philadelphia convention, was that most state constitutions had a bill of rights. Nothing in the Constitution would limit or abolish these rights. In 1788 James Madison wrote that he thought a bill of rights would provide only weak "parchment barriers" against attempts by government to take away individual rights. He believed that history had shown that a bill of rights was ineffective on "those occasions when its control [was] needed most."

The views of the Anti-Federalists seem to have had more support than did those of the Federalists. The Federalists came to realize that without a bill of rights, the states might not approve the new Constitution. To ensure ratification, the Federalists therefore agreed to support adding a bill of rights to the Constitution.

With this compromise, eleven of the thirteen states ratified the Constitution by July 1788. The new government of the United States was born. The two remaining states, North Carolina and

Rhode Island, in time accepted the new Constitution. North Carolina approved it in November 1789 and Rhode Island in May 1790.

James Madison Calls for a Bill of Rights

On April 30, 1789, George Washington took the oath of office as president. The new government was launched. One of its first jobs was to amend, or change, the Constitution to include a bill of rights. This is what many of the states had called for during the ratification process. Leading this effort in the new Congress was James Madison. He was a strong supporter of individual rights. As a member of the Virginia legislature, he had helped frame the Virginia Declaration of Rights. He had also fought for religious liberty.

Madison, however, had at first opposed including a bill of rights. But his views had changed. He feared that the Constitution would not be ratified by enough states to become law unless the Federalists offered to include a bill of rights. Madison also knew that many people were afraid of the new government. He feared they might oppose its actions or attempt to undo it. He said a bill of rights "will kill the opposition everywhere, and by putting an end to disaffection to [discontent with] the Government itself, enable the administration to venture on measures not otherwise safe."

On June 8, 1789, the thirty-eight-year-old Madison rose to speak in the House of Representatives. He called for several changes to the Constitution that contained the basis of our present Bill of Rights. Despite his powerful words, Madison's speech did not excite his listeners. Most Federalists in Congress opposed a bill of rights. Others believed that the new Constitution should be given more time to operate before Congress considered making any changes. Many Anti-Federalists wanted a new constitutional convention. There, they hoped to greatly limit the powers of the federal government. These Anti-Federalists thought that adding a bill of rights to the Constitution would prevent their movement for a new convention.

Finally, in August, Madison persuaded the House to consider

his amendments. The House accepted most of them. However, instead of being placed in the relevant sections of the Constitution, as Madison had called for, the House voted to add them as separate amendments. This change—listing the amendments together—made the Bill of Rights the distinct document that it is today.

After approval by the House, the amendments went to the Senate. The Senate dropped what Madison considered the most important part of his plan. This was the protection of freedom of the press, freedom of religious belief, and the right to trial by jury from violation by the states. Protection of these rights from violation by state governments would have to wait until after the Fourteenth Amendment was adopted in 1868.

The House and the Senate at last agreed on ten amendments to protect individual rights. What rights were protected? Here is a partial list:

The First Amendment protects freedom of religion, of speech, of the press, of peaceful assembly, and of petition.

The Second Amendment gives to the states the right to keep a militia (a volunteer, reserve military force) and to the people the right to keep and bear arms.

The Third Amendment prevents the government from keeping troops in private homes during wartime.

The Fourth Amendment protects individuals from unreasonable searches and seizures by the government.

The Fifth Amendment states that the government must get an indictment (an official ruling that a crime has been committed) before someone can be tried for a serious crime. This amendment bans "double jeopardy." This means trying a person twice for the same criminal offense. It also protects people from having to testify against themselves in court.

The Fifth Amendment also says that the government cannot take away a person's "life, liberty, or property, without due process of law." This means that the government must follow fair and just procedures if it takes away a person's "life, liberty, or property." Finally, the Fifth Amendment says that if the government takes property from an individual for public use, it must pay that person an adequate sum of money for the property.

The Sixth Amendment requires that all criminal trials be speedy and public, and decided by a fair jury. The amendment also allows people on trial to know what offense they have been charged with. It also allows them to be present when others testify against them, to call witnesses to their defense, and to have the help of a lawyer.

The Seventh Amendment provides for a jury trial in all cases involving amounts over $20.

The Eighth Amendment forbids unreasonably high bail (money paid to free someone from jail before his or her trial), unreasonably large fines, and cruel and unusual punishments.

The Ninth Amendment says that the rights of the people are not limited only to those listed in the Bill of Rights.

Finally, the Tenth Amendment helps to establish federalism by giving to the states and the people any powers not given to the federal government by the Constitution.

After being approved by the House and the Senate, the amendments were sent to the states for adoption in October 1789. By December 1791, three-fourths of the states had approved the ten amendments we now know as the Bill of Rights. The Bill of Rights had become part of the U.S. Constitution.

How Our Court System Works

Many of the events in this book concern court cases involving the Bill of Rights. To help understand how the U.S. court system works, here is a brief description.

The U.S. federal court system has three levels. At the lowest level are the federal district courts. There are ninety-four district courts, each covering a different area of the United States and its territories. Most cases having to do with the Constitution begin in the district courts.

People who lose their cases in the district courts may then appeal to the next level in the court system, the federal courts of appeals. To appeal means to take your case to a higher court in an attempt to change the lower court's decision. Here, those who are making the appeal try to obtain a different judgment. There are thirteen federal courts of appeals in the United States.

People who lose in the federal courts of appeals may then take their case to the U.S. Supreme Court. It is the highest court in the land. The Supreme Court has the final say in a case. You cannot appeal a Supreme Court decision.

The size of the Supreme Court is set by Congress and has changed over the years. Since 1869 the Supreme Court has been made up of nine justices. One is the chief justice of the United States, and eight are associate justices. The justices are named by the president and confirmed by the Senate.

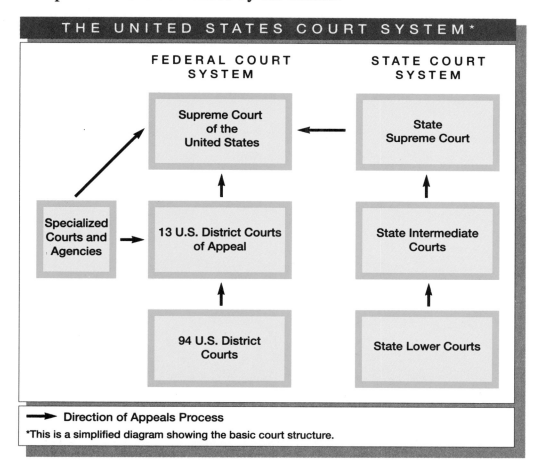

THE UNITED STATES COURT SYSTEM*

FEDERAL COURT SYSTEM — STATE COURT SYSTEM

Supreme Court of the United States ← State Supreme Court

Specialized Courts and Agencies → 13 U.S. District Courts of Appeal — State Intermediate Courts

94 U.S. District Courts — State Lower Courts

➤ Direction of Appeals Process

*This is a simplified diagram showing the basic court structure.

In the Supreme Court, a simple majority of votes is needed to decide a case. If there is a tie, the lower court's decision remains in effect. When the chief justice votes on the majority side, he or she can assign the writing of the opinion to any of the majority justices, including himself or herself. The opinion states the Court's decision and the reasons for it. Who writes the opinion when the chief justice hasn't voted on the majority side? In that case, the longest-serving associate justice who voted for the majority decision can assign the writing to any of the majority justices, including himself or herself.

What if a justice has voted for the majority decision but doesn't agree with the reasons given in the majority opinion? He or she may write what is called a concurring opinion. That is one which agrees with the Court's decision but for different reasons.

Those justices who disagree with the Court's decision may write what is called a dissenting opinion. They have the opportunity to explain why they think the majority Supreme Court decision is wrong.

In addition to the federal court system, each state has its own system of courts. These systems vary from state to state. However, they are usually made up of two or three levels of lower courts and then the state's highest court, usually called the state supreme court. Those who lose their cases in the state supreme court may appeal those decisions to the federal court system, usually to the Supreme Court.

Not all cases that are appealed to the Supreme Court are heard by it. In fact, very few of them are. For the Supreme Court to decide to hear a case, four of the nine justices must vote to hear it. If fewer than four justices vote to hear the case, then the judgment of the lower court remains in effect.

The Tenth Amendment

The Tenth Amendment stands apart from the other nine amendments. It does not directly protect citizens or name individual freedoms. Instead, it talks about the power of the government. The Constitution divides power between the federal government and the states. The Tenth Amendment reflects this. But the Tenth Amendment doesn't settle the question of exactly where all this power lies. From the beginning, the states and the federal government have struggled to take the power each felt belonged to it. The Tenth Amendment has been at the center of many of these dramatic conflicts.

PHILIP A. KLINKNER

How the Tenth Amendment Took Shape

"There is a time to sow and time to reap. We sowed our seed when we sent men to the Federal Convention. Now is the time to harvest."

JONATHAN SMITH, farmer from
western Massachusetts, January 9, 1788

A great deal of arguing went on among the delegates before the Bill of Rights was finally approved. The Anti-Federalists were terribly worried. Only fifteen years before, Americans had fought to become free of England. The control that King George and Parliament had exercised over the colonies had been too much to bear. Now, who could predict what outrageous powers the federal government might claim under the new Constitution? What if Congress waved the Constitution in one hand while it snatched everyone's rights away with the other? Some of the delegates tried to make themselves more comfortable with the new government. They fought hard for amendments that would spell out the limits of federal power. For example, a delegate from New York pushed for an amendment promising that the federal government would not ignore state constitutions. In addition, delegates from Pennsylvania, Virginia, New York, North Carolina, and Rhode Island argued for an amendment that would give the states control of their own armies.

The United States Capitol in Washington, D.C. The Constitution enumerates, or lists, many of Congress's powers. Other powers that Congress exercises are not specifically listed in the Constitution.

The Federalists, of course, saw no need for a bill of rights. In fact, many of them thought the Anti-Federalists' fears were ridiculous. How on earth could the federal government ever claim rights the Constitution did not give it? they argued. Why even bother about a bill of rights? Noah Webster, one of the Federalists, dryly suggested that any bill of rights should include a part that read:

> [E]verybody shall, in good weather, hunt on his own land, and catch fish in rivers that are public property . . . and that Congress shall never restrain any inhabitant of America from eating and drinking, at seasonable times, or prevent his lying on his left side, in a long winter's night, or even on his back, when he is fatigued by lying on his right.

Needless to say, Webster failed to convince the majority of the delegates. The first nine amendments of the Bill of Rights take individual rights very seriously. Those who hoped for a bill of rights that would support states' rights were also in for a disappointment, however. The term *states' rights* refers to the rights and powers that belong to the states, and not to the federal government. Of the first nine amendments, not one focuses mainly on states' rights.

What Makes the Tenth Amendment Different

The Tenth Amendment is different from the other amendments in several ways. For one thing, it speaks about powers rather than rights. A right is a privilege that belongs to a person. Having a right does not involve doing anything. For example, everyone has the right to be protected by the police. A power, on the other hand, involves both a right and the ability to take action. For instance, a police officer has the power to stop a suspected murderer. This means the officer has the right to back up the command to "halt" by drawing a gun.

The Tenth Amendment is also the only amendment that refers to the federal government, the states, and the people:

> The powers not delegated to the United States by the Constitution, nor prohibited by it to the States, are reserved to the States respectively [each one], or to the people.

To understand the Tenth Amendment, it is important to know that the Constitution delegates, or gives, certain powers to the federal government. Most of these powers are actually enumerated, or named. For example, the federal government has the power to set and collect taxes and to coin money. It also has the power to provide for the defense of the country and to declare war. The federal government can also regulate commerce with foreign nations and among the states. Still other powers include the power to make treaties with foreign countries and to set up courts to hear all cases arising under the Constitution.

The federal government has other powers besides those clearly listed in the Constitution. These are implied, or unstated, powers. They cover a variety of matters. The Constitution states that Congress shall "make all Laws which shall be necessary and proper for carrying into Execution the foregoing Powers and all other Powers vested by this Constitution in the Government of the United States." This "necessary and proper" clause (or elastic clause) gives the federal government the legal right to exercise the implied power that is connected to its clearly listed powers. For example, the federal government has the enumerated power to make laws concerning trade between states. That power has been stretched to include things not specifically listed in the Constitution such as regulating air, bus, train, and truck transportation between states. The federal government also regulates TV and radio. The issue of implied powers was first raised by Chief Justice John Marshall. It will be discussed in Chapter 2.

The Constitution also gives part of the federal government—the Congress—the power "to provide for the . . . general welfare of the

United States." Under this power, the federal government has done many things not listed in the Constitution. For example, the federal government has built dams and flood control projects. It has set up national parks. It has established a billion dollar system of social security benefits for older citizens and for the disabled and poor.

The States and the People

The federal government also shares certain powers with the states. These concurrent, or shared, powers include setting and collecting taxes, passing criminal laws on the same matter, and spending money for the good of the public.

The Constitution also names particular things that the states may *not* do. For instance, states may not enter into treaties with countries. Nor may states make laws that interfere with contracts or give people titles of nobility (such as "count" or "duchess"). States are also prohibited from coining money.

The states have thousands of powers. Every state creates and controls its own government and sets voting requirements for its citizens. The state controls local business, labor, and professions, as well as the ownership, use, and sale of property. The state has tremendous responsibility for looking after its citizens' health and welfare. It has the power to set and collect taxes for these purposes. Looking out for its citizens means controlling schools, hospitals, roads, and other public services. It means making laws that require vaccinations and limiting automobile exhaust fumes. It means outlawing forms of gambling and forbidding ownership of danger-ous weapons. It means establishing highway speed limits and controlling the sale and use of alcoholic beverages. It can also mean forbidding the sale of soft drinks if they are in bottles or cans that aren't accepted for return.

From the beginning, the states kept some of these important powers for themselves. After all, the Tenth Amendment says that all powers not given to the federal government or forbidden to the states are reserved to—that is, belong to—either the states or the people.

The Minnesota State Capitol in St. Paul. The Tenth Amendment did not provide the final answer to the question of exactly what powers were those solely of the states.

The Preamble, or first part, of the Constitution begins with the phrase, "We the People..." and ends with "...do ordain [officially call for] and establish this Constitution for the United States of America." *All* the powers that the Constitution of the United States gives, both to the states and to the federal government, flow directly from the people.

Now think about what the Tenth Amendment is really saying: All powers that are not given to the federal government or forbidden to the states belong either to the states or to the people. The Tenth Amendment really seems to be setting limits on the power of the federal government. Yet this is exactly what the main part of the Constitution itself does. In fact, many scholars believe that the Tenth Amendment only repeats what is said in the Constitution. If this is true, then why has the Tenth Amendment been interpreted— its meaning studied and debated—over and over again?

To answer this question, compare the wording of the Tenth Amendment with these travel directions: "Drive 14.2 miles. Turn left just before the bridge. Continue for two blocks. Stop at the bank on your right." How detailed is the amendment compared with the travel directions? Does the amendment give an exact road map for the constitutional traveler? The answer is clearly no.

Some scholars believe that those who wrote the Tenth Amendment purposely made it vague, or fuzzy. Why would they want to do that? Article II of the Articles of Confederation (ratified in 1781) will help to explain this. Article II, like the Tenth Amendment that came after it, deals with the power of state governments and the federal government. But Article II includes a key word that is not found in the Tenth Amendment. Pay special attention to the underlined word as you read the Article:

Each State retains its sovereignty [power not controlled by any other power], freedom and independence, and every power, jurisdiction and right, which is not by this confederation <u>expressly</u> delegated to the United States, in Congress assembled. [underlining added]

The word *expressly* means "directly" or "specifically." A sign in a restaurant that sets aside one area expressly for nonsmokers means "Keep out of this area if you wish to smoke!" A Congress that has only those powers expressly delegated to itself is also limited. It may do *only* those things that the Constitution actually *names* as its right. It may not do anything more. The U.S. government under the Articles of Confederation was called a body without a head. It was the word *expressly* that had chopped the head off that national body.

Those who were present at the 1787 Constitutional Convention knew how Article II of the Articles of Confederation had weakened the federal government earlier. Delegates who attended the state conventions to ratify the Constitution probably knew it, too. The word *expressly* didn't bother the Anti-Federalists. In fact, they pressed hard to have the word *expressly* included in any amendment about the "reserved powers" of the states.

After the Constitutional Convention had approved the Constitution, the states held their own conventions to make decisions about ratifying it. The Federalists had tried hard to persuade state delegates to vote for the Constitution. They convinced the delegates that amendments should be decided on separately from the Constitution itself. The states therefore came up with various ideas for amendments. Massachusetts, New Hampshire, New York, South Carolina, and Virginia all wrote amendments that reserved to the states those powers not delegated to the central government. Except for Virginia, all of these states wanted the new amendment to keep for the states all powers not "expressly," or "clearly," delegated to the federal government.

On June 8, 1789, James Madison introduced the various state amendments to Congress. His wording for the "reserved powers" amendment stated: "The powers not delegated to this constitution, nor prohibited by it to the States, are reserved to the States respectively." When the Senate approved the amendment on September 7, 1789, it included the words "or to the people." Both the

Senate and the House of Representatives accepted the amendment as the twelfth and last one. Then, after two other amendments were rejected, the ''reserved powers'' amendment moved up two places and became the tenth amendment in the list. After Congress voted to propose the ten amendments known as the Bill of Rights, it was up to the states to ratify these amendments. In 1791 the Tenth Amendment and the other nine amendments were finally ratified.

Remember, the Tenth Amendment did not include the word *expressly.* What effect would this have on the way in which the amendment was received? As you may have guessed, it left the door wide open for different interpretations of federal powers.

A Constitutional Test

In 1790, even before the Tenth Amendment was ratified, a major constitutional disagreement took place. Alexander Hamilton, the secretary of the treasury, wanted to strengthen the federal government. One of his plans was to set up a national bank. The bank would be called The Bank of the United States. It would serve many purposes. It would issue paper money. It would hold deposits of federal taxes and lend money to businesses to help them grow. It would also be the main bank for many smaller state banks. From the federal government, it would receive a charter—an official document guaranteeing and defining its rights and duties. Hamilton's plan did not please everyone.

James Madison was the leading voice that rose up against Hamilton's plan. He argued that there was nothing in the Constitution that called for a national bank. President George Washington asked for other opinions and a great debate took place.

Hamilton finally convinced Washington to go along with his plans. Hamilton argued that an act may be judged constitutional if it helps to carry out any of the powers named in the Constitution. In other words, as long as the *goal* of the act is constitutional, the methods do not actually have to be *named* in the Constitution. The first Bank of the United States was chartered for twenty years. The Constitution had been given its first test. In 1816 James Madison changed his views and, as president, supported a charter for the Second Bank of the United States.

John Marshall and National Supremacy

"Be it enacted, That the supreme court of the United States shall consist of a chief justice and five associate justices."

From the Judiciary Act of 1789

The Constitution was somewhat like an outfit that will be worn by many children in a huge and growing family. It, too, had to be flexible—able to be stretched—in order to work. The Framers had tried to create a generous document, not an unbending code of law. It soon became clear that they had succeeded. The Supreme Court (along with other federal courts) gradually began to hear and settle constitutional disagreements.

Every argument over federal and state power relates to the Tenth Amendment. Many of the Supreme Court's earliest cases involved just this kind of conflict. When these cases came before the Supreme Court, the Constitution offered very few quick answers. Most important, before the justices could settle a conflict—and Court decisions were based only on a majority vote—they had to decide which part of the Constitution applied to each problem. Happily, as the years passed, this task became easier. As more and more constitutional judgments were recorded, the Court could be guided by earlier cases. But this wasn't so in the beginning of government under the Constitution.

Chief Justice John Marshall served on the Supreme Court from 1801 to 1835. He was one of the main founders of the American system of constitutional law.

The Great John Marshall

How the Court used the Constitution to support a decision depended partly on what the justices themselves were like. This was bound to happen. When John Marshall joined the Supreme Court in 1801, the Court got one of the greatest chief justices it would ever have. Marshall served the Court for thirty-four years. During that time, Marshall's brilliant judgments helped to give lasting meaning to constitutional law. Here is a description of Marshall written just months after he took the bench:

[I]f eloquence [ability to use powerful language] may be said to consist in the power of seizing the attention with irresistible [very strong] force . . . this extraordinary man . . . deserved to be considered as one of the most eloquent men in the world. . . . He possesses one original, and, almost, supernatural faculty [ability]; the faculty of developing a subject by a single glance of his mind, and detecting at once, the very point on which each controversy depends. No matter what the question; though ten times more knotty than the gnarled oak, the lightning of heaven is not more rapid nor more resistless, than his astonishing penetration [ability to know and understand deeply].

Marbury v. *Madison*

Marshall's gifts first became widely known in the case of *Marbury* v. *Madison* (1803). Marshall was the judge in this legal dispute. He was also the person who had set the dispute in motion. In 1800 Marshall had been the secretary of state under President John Adams. Adams was a loyal Federalist in a nation where feelings between Federalists and Anti-Federalists ran high. Adams had just been defeated by the Republican Thomas Jefferson in the election for president. Before leaving office, Adams signed two acts of Congress. Among other things, the acts created several new judgeships that could be filled with Federalist judges. Adams spent his last night as president signing the commissions of his "midnight judges." A commission is a special government document giving a person the power to hold a government office.

As outgoing secretary of state, it was John Marshall's job to deliver the commissions. Marshall failed to deliver some of them and left them in his desk. Among these was the one that would have appointed William Marbury as justice of the peace in the District of Columbia. When James Madison, the new secretary of state, found the commissions in the desk drawer, he told President Jefferson. The two men decided to go ahead as if Madison had never opened that drawer. Madison did not deliver the commissions.

Marbury, who had been expecting his commission, wasn't willing to let the matter drop. He filed a lawsuit with the Supreme Court. He asked the Court to issue a special order known as a writ of mandamus. A writ of mandamus orders a government official to do his or her duty. Such an order would force Madison to hand over the commission to Marbury.

John Marshall was by then the chief justice of the United States. He found himself in a sticky situation. What should his decision in this case be? If he went along with Marbury, the result might be bad. President Jefferson and Secretary of State Madison were both political enemies of John Adams. They might ignore Marshall's decision. The Supreme Court has no enforcement powers (these belong to the executive branch). If the executive branch ignored the Court's decision, that would be awful for the reputation of the Court. If, however, Chief Justice Marshall rejected Marbury's claim, that, too, would make the Court seem weak. After all, the Judiciary Act of 1789 said the Supreme Court could issue writs of mandamus. Marshall therefore gave the various sides of the problem careful thought. Then he made his decision.

Marshall's opinion showed him to be a gifted problem solver. He had to ask and answer many questions before he could deliver a decision. Did Marbury have a legal right to the commission?

William Marbury, whom President John Adams had appointed justice of the peace in the District of Columbia. But when Thomas Jefferson became president, the secretary of state, James Madison, withheld the document of appointment. The case that resulted—*Marbury* v. *Madison* (1803)—was one of the most important in the history of the United States.

Marshall said that he did indeed. Was Marbury's demand for a writ of mandamus proper? Marshall agreed that it certainly was. Marshall then raised the central question in this dispute: Should the Supreme Court issue this writ? No, Marshall said. Although the Judiciary Act of 1789 gave the Court this power, the Constitution did not. The Constitution is fundamental, or first, law. For this reason, Marshall concluded, this part of the Judiciary Act must be unconstitutional. So, far from weakening the Supreme Court, Marshall had given it the power to declare an act of Congress unconstitutional. This power to review the laws and actions of other parts of government is known as judicial review. Marshall had shown the Court's power to review the actions of the other branches of the federal government.

Fletcher v. *Peck*

In 1810 Marshall and the Court heard another major case, *Fletcher* v. *Peck*. That case involved a lawsuit that some settlers had brought against the state of Georgia. A dishonest Georgia legislature had earlier sold millions of acres of land along the Yazoo River to land companies. These companies in turn had sold off bits of the land to the settlers. The profits made by the land companies were enormous. However, in 1796 the next state legislature decided to repeal, or cancel, the land grant that the earlier government had made. But those who had paid precious money for their small parcels of land were determined to keep what they had bought.

When the case reached the highest court, the Supreme Court ruled that Georgia did have the right to make the original land grant. The Court then stated that it would be unconstitutional to repeal that grant. Marshall saw the grant as a contract. He therefore used the contract clause (in Article I, Section 10 of the Constitution) to support the Court's decision: "No State shall . . . pass any . . . Law impairing the Obligation of Contracts. . . ."

Some scholars question whether the Framers of the Constitution would have thought of land grants to companies as contracts. Nevertheless, *Fletcher* v. *Peck* (1810) helped to both call attention to and support contract rights. More important, the case marked the first time that a state law was declared by the Supreme Court to be unconstitutional. (The Court had several times previously forbidden state laws that conflicted with federal laws and treaties.)

Martin v. *Hunter's Lessee*

In 1816 the case of *Martin* v. *Hunter's Lessee* came before the Supreme Court. This legal conflict involved the ownership of land in Virginia. Hunter claimed that the land in question had been given to him by the state of Virginia. (Virginia had a law that permitted the state to take land away from people who had been on the side of the British during the American Revolution. The land was then given to people like Hunter.) Martin, too, claimed the land and refused to give up his claim to it. He explained that his family had owned the land even before the Revolution. Martin pointed to a federal treaty that made it unlawful for Virginia to take the land.

The Virginia Supreme Court had ruled in Hunter's favor twice before the case went to the Supreme Court. Virginia now presented its argument to Marshall: If a case began in a state court, the U.S. Supreme Court had no right to overturn that court's decision. The state's highest court should have the final word.

Under Chief Justice Marshall, the Supreme Court rejected Virginia's argument. It ruled that the Supreme Court had the right to decide the constitutionality of a ruling made by the highest court of any state in the land. This Supreme Court decision established one of the Court's most important powers: the power to review state court decisions.

Thus, case by case, Marshall upheld what he saw as the powers of the federal government over the states.

McCullough v. *Maryland*

In 1819 Marshall handed down another major decision. The case was *McCullough* v. *Maryland*. McCullough was a cashier in a branch of the Second Bank of the United States in Baltimore, Maryland. The Second Bank of the United States had been set up by the federal government in 1816. Its central office was in Philadelphia. It had branches around the country. Many people disliked having a national bank in their midst. They felt that the federal government had gone too far in establishing a national bank in the first place. The state of Maryland passed an antinational bank law. It also taxed banks not chartered by the state. When Maryland asked McCullough to pay this tax, he refused. Maryland, as the

The Second Bank of the United States had its central office in Philadelphia. In 1819, the Supreme Court ruled unanimously that Congress had the power to charter the bank. The Court declared unconstitutional the Maryland state law that taxed the national bank.

plaintiff (the party that brings a legal action, complains, or sues) first sued McCullough in a state court. The court ruled in favor of Maryland. The Second Bank of the United States then brought an appeal before the Supreme Court.

The Court had to decide on two vital questions in the case of *McCullough* v. *Maryland:* Is it legal for the United States to establish a national bank? Does a state have the right to tax a federal bank? The first question had come up in 1790, when Alexander Hamilton first established a national bank. It was clear that the Constitution says nothing about the federal government establishing banks. But, like Hamilton, Marshall took a broad view of the Constitution. He asked whether the Constitution was in fact "an act of sovereign and independent States" or a document from and for the American people. He decided that the "Government of the Union . . . is emphatically [definitely] . . . a government of the people. . . . [T]he government of the Union, though limited in its powers, is supreme within the sphere of its action." Marshall therefore supported the belief in what is called national sovereignty. (*Sovereignty* means power that is uncontrolled by any other power.) The federal government's power came from the people of the states, not from the states as governing bodies.

Marshall supported his conclusions with words from the Constitution: "The people have in express terms decided it by saying: 'This Constitution and the laws of the United States which shall be made in pursuance thereof [to uphold the Constitution] . . . shall be the supreme Law of the Land.'" This is the supremacy clause.

Marshall claimed that the Constitution gave Congress the power to make all laws "necessary and proper" for carrying out the powers of the government. This claim was based on the "necessary and proper" clause of Article I, Section 8, of the Constitution. The lawyers for Maryland argued that "necessary" meant "absolutely necessary." Marshall argued back that in his view, "necessary" had a much looser meaning. The word, he said, appears "in a Constitution intended to endure for ages to come and consequently to be adapted to the various crises of human affairs." Therefore, it was decided, Congress has the right to choose any methods needed to carry out its powers well. Even though the Constitution did not list the setting up of a bank as one of the powers of Congress, it was an implied power. Implied powers are those not stated in so many words. But they are necessary and proper to carry out various clearly stated powers.

Next, Marshall ruled against a state's right to tax a federal bank. His decision established the principle that no state may tax the federal government. As part of his forceful argument, Marshall said: "The power to tax involves the power to destroy . . . the power to destroy may defeat and render [make] useless the power [of the federal government] to create." Marshall also stated that the issue here was really that of deciding upon the highest law of the land. If states were given the right to tax the federal government, Marshall said, "the declaration that the Constitution and the laws . . . shall be supreme law of the land . . . is empty." (Later, in 1832, President Andrew Jackson refused to give the bank a new charter. The bank was supposed to have its charter renewed by 1836 at the latest. Jackson had decided that a national bank was unconstitutional.)

In *Marbury* v. *Madison* (1803), *Fletcher* v. *Peck* (1810), and *McCullough* v. *Maryland* (1819), Marshall had found support in the Constitution for striking down a congressional act, a state law, and a state action. In handing down the Court's decisions, Marshall pointed to the contract clause, the necessary and proper clause, and the supremacy clause of the Constitution. In *Martin* v. *Hunter's Lessee* (1816), the Supreme Court established its right to review state court decisions.

Gibbons v. *Ogden*

A few years after *McCullough* v. *Maryland*, Marshall spoke of the commerce clause of the Constitution for the first time. This clause would play a major part in Tenth Amendment issues from then on.

The seeds for the important case of *Gibbons* v. *Ogden* (1824) had been planted by inventor Robert Fulton and his backer, Robert Livingston. Fulton had seen steamboats in Europe. Back in the United States, he experimented until he had perfected a commercial model. Then, with the help of his backer, Robert Livingston,

In 1807 Robert Fulton built the *Clermont,* the first commercially successful steamboat to sail the Hudson River. In 1815, the ship was dismantled. However, Robert Fulton and Robert Livingston's monopoly to sail steamboats on the Hudson continued. These were the rights that Aaron Ogden obtained and that led to the famous Supreme Court battle of *Gibbons* v. *Ogden* (1824).

Fulton put together a steamboat. In 1808 Livingston and Fulton got from the New York State legislature the right to have the only company allowed to navigate the steamships along the Hudson River. Needless to say, the two men made an excellent profit.

Years later, Thomas Gibbons obtained a license from the United States to operate steamboats in the "coasting trade." Gibbons then ran a commercial vessel in the waters of the Hudson River between the states of New Jersey and New York. Aaron Ogden held a license from the Fulton-Livingston company. Ogden challenged Gibbons's rights. A New York State court ordered Gibbons to stop running his boats in New York waters. Gibbons then pleaded his case before the U.S. Supreme Court. He said that the state did not have the right to grant a monopoly, or exclusive right, to anyone. He argued that navigation is commerce among the several states and that Congress had the power to regulate that commerce.

The question of trade and business between states—interstate commerce—has been an important issue in constitutional law. Does commerce involve only buying and selling or does it include navigation? How great is Congress's power to control interstate commerce? Can states have a concurrent right? That is, can the federal government and a state government have the same right?

In *Gibbons* v. *Ogden*, Marshall ruled in favor of Gibbons and against the state. The Supreme Court forbade New York State from ordering Gibbons to stop running his boats in New York waters. Marshall said that commerce included every kind of "commercial intercourse." He held that a trip that begins in one state and ends in another was subject to federal laws every mile of the way. Marshall stated that Congress's power over interstate commerce was "complete in itself, may be exercised to its utmost extent, and acknowledges no limitations other than are prescribed in the Constitution."

Gibbons won his case. But Marshall did not base the Court's decision on the commerce clause. Instead, he pointed to the federal law that gave people the right to use the nation's waterways. *Gibbons* v. *Ogden* (1824) was a landmark case, one that would be pointed to by the Supreme Court again and again in years to come.

Among other things, this case helped to establish the Constitution as the supreme law of the land.

Barron v. *The Mayor and City Council of Baltimore*

One more case needs to be mentioned—John Marshall's last important one. In 1833 Marshall wrote an opinion about *Barron* v. *The Mayor and City Council of Baltimore*. The Court was unanimous—that is, all the justices voted for the decision. The basis for the case was laid when Baltimore, Maryland, began paving some of its streets. Certain streams were redirected from their natural path. One—near Barron's Wharf—became clogged with sand and gravel. John Barron's wharf, which until then had been able to accept vessels, was now useless. Barron went to court. He accused Baltimore of violating a part of the Fifth Amendment of the Constitution. He was referring to the section that forbids the use of private property "for public use without just compensation [payment]." Barron won his argument. But Baltimore appealed to the Maryland State Court of Appeals. There the decision was overturned. Barron then appealed to the U.S. Supreme Court.

The Supreme Court's decision, written by Marshall, was clear. "Had the framers of the Amendments [the ten that make up the Bill of Rights] intended them to be limitations on the powers of the state governments, they would have . . . expressed that intention . . . in plain and intelligible language." The protections of the Bill of Rights were protections against the federal government, not against actions taken by state governments. Marshall went on to say that "the fifth amendment must be understood as restraining the power of the general government, not as applicable to [applying to] the States." Barron lost his case. Not until 1868 would cases like this be seen in a different light.

One hundred years after Marshall left the bench, Supreme Court Justice Benjamin Cardozo wrote the following:

Marshall gave to the Constitution of the United States the impress [stamp or special mark] of his own mind; and the form of our constitutional law is what it is, because he moulded it while it was still plastic and malleable [soft enough to be shaped] in the fire of his own intense convictions.

CHAPTER 3

States' Rights, Roger Taney, and Dual Federalism

"In respect to civil rights, common to all citizens, the Constitution . . .
does not . . . permit any public authority to know the race of those
entitled to be protected in the enjoyment of such rights."

JUSTICE JOHN HARLAN, dissenting in *Plessy* v. *Ferguson* (1896)

Since the nation's beginnings, there have always been strong
forces that tried to draw power to the states. Most states' rights
supporters have shared the same goal: to protect the rights and
powers of the states. Those who favor states' rights believe in
keeping the federal government from taking over the powers
reserved to the states. Even today, states continue to raise the
question of states' rights whenever they feel that their rights are in
danger.

Kentucky and Virginia Resolutions

An early expression of states' rights was the Kentucky and Virginia
Resolutions. These resolutions were written by Thomas Jefferson
and James Madison in 1798 and 1799. The resolutions were then
passed by those two state legislatures. The Kentucky and Virginia
Resolutions were written in response to several laws that Congress
had passed. The laws were known as the Alien and Sedition Acts.

Roger B. Taney, as U.S. attorney general and U.S. secretary of the treasury,
opposed the Second Bank of the United States. He served as chief justice of
the United States from 1836 to 1864. Taney's most famous majority opinion
was the ruling that favored slavery in the *Dred Scott* case (1857).

Among other things, the Sedition Act forbade writing, printing, or publishing "any false, scandalous and malicious" material that criticized either Congress or the president. This law attempted to keep people from speaking out about government activities and plans. It made freedom of speech and freedom of the press punishable under certain circumstances. Freedom of speech and freedom of the press are among the rights guaranteed by the First Amendment. The law did not actually censor, or try to stop the press. But it opened the way for punishment if objectionable material was printed.

Jefferson and Madison declared that the Alien and Sedition Acts were unconstitutional. Madison wrote that the states "have a right and are in duty bound to interpose [step in] for arresting [stopping] the progress of the evil." The resolutions said that the states were the best judges of what acts were unconstitutional. Furthermore, a majority of states had the right to join together to nullify, or cancel, such laws. Accordingly, the states rather than any branch of the federal government should have the right to declare laws unconstitutional. Other states did not support this theory of nullification.

The Hartford Convention

Years later the demands for states' rights appeared in the Northeast during the War of 1812. The War of 1812 was being fought between the United States and Great Britain. Many states were against this war. Some Americans even sided with the British. Massachusetts had called for a secret meeting of state delegates in Hartford, Connecticut. The reason for the Hartford Convention of 1814 was to discuss complaints and make plans for safety. Some delegates were so angry that they were ready to urge their states to break away from the Union. The majority were calmer, however. The delegates introduced a resolution. It stated that when an act of Congress went against the Constitution, a state had "not only the right but the duty . . . to interpose its authority for . . . protection, in the best manner calculated to secure that end." The states had wanted to present their views to Congress. But the war ended before they could do so.

National Protective Tariffs

Still another controversial federal action that stirred up the issue of states' rights was a national protective tariff. A protective tariff is a duty—an extra tax or charge—added to the cost of imports, or goods that are brought into a country. In 1816 Congress and President James Madison approved a tariff to raise the price of foreign goods. The tariff was designed to protect U.S. industries against foreign competition. Protected items included woolen, cotton, and iron products as well as paper, leather, and hats.

People in different states took different positions on the tariff question. Opinion of those in the New England states was mixed. Senator Daniel Webster was against the tariff. He supported shipping interests and wanted free overseas trade. On the other hand, many statesmen were in favor of the tariff. States in the West and the Middle Atlantic region voted for the tariff. John Calhoun, from South Carolina, was also for it. Calhoun had been vice-president of the United States since 1825. He hoped the tariff would help the manufacturing that some in the South planned to develop. But manufacturing didn't develop in the South as well as Southerners had hoped it would. Southerners came to feel that a tariff on foreign goods hurt the South while helping New England.

In 1828 Congress approved another, even higher tariff. This time Calhoun was against it. He secretly wrote a paper for the South Carolina legislature. The legislature issued the *South Carolina Exposition and Protest.* The paper pointed out that the Constitution gave the federal government power to set up tariffs for *income,* but not for *protection.* It declared that the tariff was unconstitutional. The paper also pointed out that the states had the right of interposition. Interposition was a state's right to reject any law passed by Congress or any action of the federal government that it believed was unconstitutional or went beyond the powers given to Congress by the Constitution. According to this principle, if federal actions conflict with state laws, all people in the state should obey the state law.

Calhoun then described a method by which a state could nullify a federal law or action. Nullification could go into effect, he reasoned, if a special state convention declared the federal law or action null and void because it violated the Constitution. Calhoun believed that the process of nullification would be better than secession—a state leaving the Union.

The Webster-Hayne Debate

The states' rights ideas of nullification and interposition soon became an issue again. In 1830 these ideas were used by Senator Robert Hayne of South Carolina in his Senate debate with Senator Daniel Webster of Massachusetts. The Webster-Hayne debate was over whether or not the sale of public western lands should be limited. Hayne used Calhoun's ideas to strengthen his views in favor of a policy providing cheap land in the West. He said that a state had the right to nullify an act of Congress if it went against the Constitution. Webster, however, argued that nullification would destroy the Union. "Liberty *and* Union, now and forever, one and inseparable!" he declared.

Nullification and the Force Act of 1833

In 1832 Congress passed another tariff act. At a special state convention, South Carolina then passed an ordinance. This ordinance was a special decree and law that made these tariffs null and void in South Carolina. It forbade the collection of the federal tariffs in the state. The state threatened to secede from the Union if the tariff laws were carried out. At this point President Andrew Jackson wanted to make it clear that federal laws would be enforced. He issued a Nullification Proclamation that declared nullification an "impractical absurdity." Jackson then sent ships and troop reinforcements to South Carolina. In the meantime,

Calhoun was elected to represent South Carolina in the Senate. He then resigned as vice president in order to become a senator.

At President Jackson's request, Congress passed the Force Act of 1833 to uphold his position. The Force Act said the army should be used to force South Carolina to comply with federal law. At the same time Congress passed a new, compromise bill—one that lowered the tariffs that South Carolina had resisted. The special state convention in South Carolina then canceled its nullification of the federal government's earlier high tariff law. There was no longer a need to use federal troops to enforce the tariffs. Soon after that, the friction between Jackson and South Carolina died down.

Roger B. Taney as Chief Justice

Roger B. Taney (pronounced TAW-nee) replaced John Marshall as chief justice of the United States in 1836. It was then that Marshall's friend Senator Daniel Webster wrote these grim words: "Judge Story [a Supreme Court justice] thinks the Supreme Court is *gone* and I think so too."

From a Federalist point of view, Taney's appointment might well have turned out to be a disaster. After all, Taney had been appointed to the Court by President Andrew Jackson. Jackson was an enthusiastic Democrat and a champion of states' rights. A Taney Court could be expected to be on the side of local rather than national interests.

Webster's fears were largely unfounded, however. Taney actually shared some of Marshall's views. He handed down many rulings that strengthened the idea of judicial control. At the same time, the Taney Court delivered many rulings that supported states' rights. In fact, looking back, it is clear that the part of the Tenth Amendment that speaks of the reserved powers of the states was as important to Taney as the supremacy clause had been to Marshall. Taney's ideas about government have been called dual federalism. Under dual federalism, the federal and state governments are each sovereign, or in charge, in their own areas.

During his twenty-nine years on the bench, Taney examined

many cases that dealt with constitutional issues. We will look at just a few of these cases. One involved contract agreements, and four had to do with the commerce power. In each of these cases, the Supreme Court made its decision in an effort to make the Constitution work for a growing nation. Still another case stands alone. It is the *Dred Scott* decision. The case that is officially called *Dred Scott* v. *Sandford* (1857) was to leave a stain on Roger Taney's name.

Charles River Bridge v. *Warren Bridge*

The basis for the case dealing with contracts, the *Charles River Bridge* v. *Warren Bridge* case, was laid in 1785. In that year the Massachusetts state legislature incorporated—that is, formed into a corporation—the Charles River Bridge Company. The state law-making body gave the company the go-ahead to build the Charles River Bridge connecting Boston and Charlestown. The charter, or special agreement, between the two parties would last forty years. Earlier, the state had given Harvard College the rights for running a ferry across the Charles River. Now the tolls for using the new bridge would be handed over to Harvard.

Tolls were paid, and the business was a great success. In 1792 the state gave the charter another thirty years to run. Then, in 1828, the state legislature chartered another company to build the Warren Bridge. The two bridges would be less than 300 yards apart! According to this plan, the Warren Bridge Company would accept tolls only until its building costs were paid for. After that, bridge travel would be free to everyone.

Not surprisingly, the owners of the Charles River Bridge Company weren't pleased. They asked the state court for an injunction, or legal order, against the building of the Warren Bridge. The request for an injunction was turned down. In 1837 the case went to the Supreme Court for review. The owners of the Charles River Bridge insisted that their charter was a contract. They felt that a contract would protect their right to be the only bridge operators in the area. The new state legislation, they charged, was unconstitutional. They felt that it violated the contract clause of the U.S. Constitution. True, the charter did not say in so many words that the Charles River Company had the only rights. But wasn't the charter meant to be understood as giving the company all the rights that might belong to it?

The lawyers for the Warren Bridge Company argued that the state had a right to make laws for the public good. They held that corporate, or business, charters should protect only those rights that are named directly.

Boston at about the time that the Supreme Court ruled on the *Charles Street Bridge* v. *Warren Bridge* case in 1837.

Chief Justice Roger B. Taney ruled in favor of the Warren Bridge. In his opinion, he wrote:

> The object and end of all government is to promote the happiness and prosperity of the community by which it is established. . . . And in a country like ours . . . continually advancing in numbers and wealth; new channels of communication are daily found necessary, both for travel and trade . . . the interests of the great body of the people of the State, would, in this instance, be affected by the surrender of this great line of travel to a single corporation, with the right to exact [call for and obtain] toll, and exclude competition for seventy years. . . . We cannot take away from them [the states] any portion of that power over their own internal police and improvement, which is so necessary to their well-being and prosperity.

The phrase "power over their own internal police" is a key one. The police power referred to does not mean the power of a police officer on patrol. The police power of a state refers to the state's legal right to protect its citizens. This right covers the areas of health, welfare, safety, and morals, both through laws and in other ways. The police power also plays an important role in each of the following three landmark cases.

Mayor of New York v. *Miln*

Mayor of New York v. *Miln* came before the Court in 1837. The case grew out of a dispute between New York and a ship's officer named Miln. According to New York law, ships' masters had to give certain information about the passengers they brought into port. This time a ship's officer—Miln—refused to do so. The state law was attacked. Miln's lawyers claimed that it interfered with Congress's power over foreign commerce. The Court might have ruled that Congress has complete power over commerce. On the other hand, it might have decided that the states had the right to control all interstate and foreign commerce *unless* a state law interfered with a federal act or law. The Court did neither of these things. Instead, it upheld the state law without basing the ruling on the commerce clause. The Court said the state law represented legal use of the state's police powers. The New York law, said the Court, was clearly meant to protect the state's own welfare.

Arguing against the ruling, the lawyers for the plaintiff pointed to *Gibbons* v. *Ogden* (1824)—the steamship monopoly case heard by John Marshall. Didn't that decision give Congress complete power over interstate and foreign commerce? they asked. No, said the Court. The two cases were different. In *Gibbons* v. *Ogden,* the state law clashed with an act of Congress. In this case there was no particular act of Congress that could interfere with the state law.

In spite of the Court's ruling in *Mayor of New York* v. *Miln* (1837), serious questions still remained. In the absence of federal commerce laws, the states had passed many regulations having to do with commerce. Other cases would surely come up. How could the Court decide whether a state's reason for passing a law was to protect its citizens or to regulate commerce? The Court would soon have to deal with more than a state's police power. It would have to look at the state's right to regulate commerce.

The *Licence* Cases and *Passenger* Cases

The 1847 *License* cases involved laws of New Hampshire, Massachusetts, and Rhode Island that taxed liquor that had been imported from out of state. The basis for the case was one side's claim that taxing imported liquor was unconstitutional. Each member of the Supreme Court had his own opinion on the matter. Finally, however, the Court handed down a decision that upheld the states' laws. The majority of the justices agreed that the laws were another example of the state's use of its police power.

In 1849 the Supreme Court heard the *Passenger* cases. These cases dealt with New York and Massachusetts laws that taxed foreign passengers who arrived in state ports. Again, the Court's ruling upheld state law. And again, the justices held a variety of opinions to support the Court's ruling.

Cooley v. *Board of Wardens of the Port of Philadelphia*

In the three earlier cases, it was the police power, not the commerce power, that was the basis for the Court's decisions. Two important questions remained unanswered. First, could the commerce power be held concurrently, that is, by both the federal government and the states? Second, could the states regulate interstate or foreign commerce if there was still no specific federal regulation? In 1851 the case of *Cooley* v. *Board of Wardens of the Port of Philadelphia* brought these issues into sharper focus. This case concerned ships that sailed in or out of the port of Philadelphia. Cooley was a shipowner who used the port. He objected to having to follow state regulations about pilots and fees for ships that were engaged in interstate or foreign commerce. Cooley refused to pay.

This time the Supreme Court's opinion would offer practical guidelines for the future. The Court made it clear that the word *commerce* covered many matters. Some were national and called for congressional action. Here only the federal government had power. But other features of commerce were local. These called for local regulations. For example, a state can require that only a state-licensed pilot may bring a foreign ship all the way into a local port or harbor. In this case the pilot boards the ship and takes over for the ship's captain. Another example is that some states have their own regulations for protecting the environment. Such states may have laws that limit a factory's dumping of acids and poisons into state waters.

In the case of *Cooley* v. *Board of Wardens of the Port of Philadelphia* (1851), the Court ruled that the states and the federal government had concurrent powers. The Court said the states could pass laws as long as they didn't go against existing federal legislation. In other words, states had limited concurrent power over interstate commerce in cases where Congress had not yet acted. The Supreme Court held that the regulation of pilots is best done by state regulation. Cooley therefore lost his suit.

These commerce decisions are revealing. They show how much the Taney Court respected both the *supremacy* of the federal government and the *reserved powers* of the states. However, Taney's dual federalist approach finally worked against the Union.

The Northern and Southern states came into more and more serious conflict during the time Taney was chief justice—from 1836 to 1864. The problems were complicated. But the main issue that would threaten to destroy the Union was slavery. In 1850 a great debate took place in Congress. The result was the Compromise of 1850, designed to keep some kind of balance between free states and slave states in the Union. As the North-South struggle grew, Taney moved toward a strong position of state sovereignty. (State sovereignty means state power that is not controlled by any other power.) Taney believed in the Union. But he also believed that the Constitution supported the South's "peculiar institution"—slavery.

The *Dred Scott* Decision

When the *Dred Scott* case (*Dred Scott* v. *Sandford*) came before the Supreme Court in 1857, Taney and some of his fellow justices were glad. Here was a chance to decide national policy and help solve the slavery issue. The Court's judgment would never be more mistaken.

Dred Scott, a slave, first sued for his freedom in the Missouri state courts. His suit was based on a number of facts. Scott had belonged to Dr. John Emerson, an army surgeon. Emerson took Scott to live outside of the slave state of Missouri. They went first to the free state of Illinois and then to the territory of Wisconsin (now a part of Minnesota), where an act of Congress known as the Missouri Compromise of 1820 had outlawed slavery. Later Emerson returned to Missouri with Scott. Then, when Emerson died, the ownership of Scott passed on to a New Yorker named John Sandford.

Scott's case rested on his claim that he had a right, as a citizen of Missouri, to sue a citizen of another state. He had become a citizen, explained his lawyer, because he had lived in a free state and in a free territory. Although Scott won in the lower courts, the Missouri Supreme Court rejected his plea. Next, Scott appealed to a federal court and lost again. It was then that he took his case to the U.S. Supreme Court.

The Supreme Court ruled that Dred Scott was still a slave. As such, he did not have the right to sue. In Taney's opinion, the Founding Fathers had not meant for any African American, slave or free, to become a U.S. citizen. Therefore, even if Scott had been made a citizen of a state, he could never become an American citizen.

Taney's argument went further. In writing the Court's opinion, Taney said the following:

> [I]f the Constitution recognized the right of property of the master in a slave, and makes no distinction between that description of property and other property owned by a citizen, no tribunal [court] acting under the authority of the United States . . . has a right to draw such a distinction, or to deny to it the benefit . . . for the protection of private property against the encroachments of [the seizure by] the government.

According to Taney, a slave was property. Property was protected by the Constitution. Slaves, then, could be taken anywhere in the United States, even to free states. They would still be protected property.

In the North, the *Dred Scott* decision landed like a bombshell. Taney's opinion strengthened the position of those who supported slavery. It also meant that even communities that were against slavery had to accept slaves as property. The *Dred Scott* decision brought the Union that much closer to the time when it would be torn apart by civil war.

The Civil War

The issue of states' rights was carried as far as it could possibly go in 1860 and 1861. It was during that period that eleven Southern states seceded from the Union. The states formed what is called the Confederate States of America. Jefferson Davis was elected president of the Confederate states. Some Confederates were really Union people who were just in the wrong place at the wrong time. Others were fiery supporters of states' rights. The most extreme supporters of states' rights even opposed the central power of the Confederate government. (Within a couple years they even questioned the right of the Confederacy to draft people into the army and to tax farm produce.)

In April 1861 Confederate forces fired on Fort Sumter. This marked the beginning of the Civil War. The North and the South fought for four terrible years. When the South was finally defeated, it was clear that the federal government was again supreme. States' rights never again had quite the same meaning.

The Birth of the Fourteenth Amendment and Its Relationship to the Tenth Amendment

Life for newly freed African Americans was difficult at best. Black Codes created by the Southern states drastically limited what former slaves could do. For example, certain rules forced African Americans into long, unrewarding apprenticeships, or work arrangements. Other codes set up racial discrimination in schools and other public places. The penalties for breaking the codes were stricter for blacks than were penalties for similar "crimes" by whites.

Before the Fourteenth Amendment, there had been other serious efforts to give African Americans their rightful privileges. In January 1863, as the Civil War raged, President Abraham Lincoln's previously announced Emancipation Proclamation went into effect. He had declared that in most of the Confederate states, persons kept as slaves "are, and henceforth shall be, free." The ratification of the Thirteenth Amendment, in 1865, actually made slavery illegal. Soon after that, the Civil Rights Act of 1866 forbade "discrimination in civil rights or immunities . . . on account of race." African Americans were declared citizens and were granted equal rights. Any person found guilty of depriving citizens of their rights because of race, color, or previous condition of servitude could be fined up to $1,000, imprisoned, or both. U.S. federal courts would handle cases involving violations of the Civil Rights Act of 1866.

The Fourteenth Amendment contains many of the guidelines of the Civil Rights Act of 1866. The first sentence of the amendment relates directly to the *Dred Scott* decision:

> All persons born or naturalized in the United States, and subject to the jurisdiction [legal power] thereof, are citizens of the United States and of the State wherein they reside.

These words defined American citizenship for the first time. They gave African Americans both national and state citizenship.

The rest of Section 1 of the amendment is a guarantee of individual liberties:

No State shall make or enforce any law which shall abridge [cut short] the <u>privileges or immunities</u> of citizens of the United States; nor shall any State deprive any person of life, liberty, or property, <u>without due process of law;</u> nor deny to any person within its jurisdiction <u>the equal protection of the laws.</u> [underlining added]

The phrases that are underlined here turned out to be as important as they are general. Together, these words have raised more questions than has any other part of the Constitution. One example is the phrase "privileges and immunities," which also appears in Article IV, Section 2 of the Constitution. It refers to the rights and protections given to American citizens. Some of the men who wrote the Fourteenth Amendment hoped that this and the other key words would help to protect people such as African Americans from abuses by various states.

How does the Fourteenth Amendment relate to the Tenth Amendment? The connection will soon become clear. But first it is important to remember that the original Bill of Rights had been interpreted as a protection of the people from abuses by the federal government only. The Bill of Rights at that time did not apply to the actions of state and local governments. People had to look to their state constitutions and state bills of rights for such protection.

When John Barron sued Baltimore for ruining his wharf in 1833 (*Barron* v. *The Mayor and City Council of Baltimore*), he based his appeal on the Fifth Amendment:

No person . . . [shall be] deprived of life, liberty, or property, without due process of law; nor shall private property be taken for public use without just compensation.

Barron argued that the guarantees named in the Fifth Amendment applied to the states as well as the federal government. Chief Justice John Marshall and the Supreme Court disagreed:

Rights cases (1883), the Supreme Court ruled 8 to 1 against them. The Court said that the guarantees of equal protection and due process given by the Fourteenth Amendment applied only to state action. *State action* has to do with the conduct of a state government or any of its subdivisions. These include cities, counties, and so forth. The Court pointed to the Fourteenth Amendment's wording: "No State shall make or enforce any law. . . ." The Fourteenth Amendment did not protect against discrimination by a private group such as an inn or theater, according to the Court's narrow interpretation of the Fourteenth Amendment. Furthermore, the Court ruled that the Fourteenth Amendment did not give Congress the power to regulate private conduct. The only lawmaking power given to Congress by the Fourteenth Amendment was the power to pass laws to prevent *states,* by their own actions, from interfering with civil rights. Therefore, the Court ruled, the Civil Rights Act of 1875 was unconstitutional. This 1883 Court decision resulted in the end of Congress's efforts to stop racial segregation until the 1940s.

The *Slaughter-House* Cases

Even before Reconstruction ended in 1877, the Fourteenth Amendment began to be applied—or at least thought about—in an unexpected way. The *Slaughter-House* cases involved a Louisiana state law. This law gave one New Orleans company a monopoly to slaughter all livestock in that city. This drove other local butchers out of business. Many butchers were understandably upset.

Before the Fourteenth Amendment, the butchers would have no constitutional grounds for complaint. Now, the Fourteenth Amendment might give them a chance. Perhaps it would keep the state government from interfering in their business. Some of these butchers therefore fought the law in the courts. They claimed that it took away their "privileges and immunities" as Louisiana citizens.

One brilliant former Supreme Court justice, John Campbell, argued for the butchers. He spoke of the rights of man—that is, people's basic rights—that were now under federal protection. He insisted that freedom to work was one of these rights.

The majority of the justices felt differently, however. They voted 5 to 4 against the butchers and in favor of the state law. Justice Samuel F. Miller presented the Supreme Court's majority opinion. The Court said that the Fourteenth Amendment discussed both U.S. citizenship and state citizenship. "Fundamental" rights such as the butchers' right to practice their trade were under the power of the states, not the federal government. If the state of Louisiana did not want to protect such rights, there was nothing the federal government should or could do. The Fourteenth Amendment's privileges and immunities clause, the majority said, didn't refer to state citizenship. It referred only to the privileges of national citizenship. Also, according to the Court, these privileges included only a few things, such as the right to use seaports and federal protection "when on the high seas." Only these limited rights did the federal government protect from state actions.

In handing down the ruling in the *Slaughter-House* cases (1873), the Court took the muscle right out of the immunities and privileges clause of the amendment. The Court's decision had again limited the protections given to the federal government by the Bill of Rights. It left the states free to ignore people's individual liberties. It also gave the federal government little power to protect African Americans from state and local abuses.

Yet the dissenting opinion in this case would prove to be extremely important. Justice Joseph P. Bradley said, "In my view, a law which prohibits a large class of citizens from adopting a lawful employment . . . does deprive them of liberty as well as property, without due process of law. . . . Such a law also deprives those citizens of the equal protection of the law." In other words, Bradley believed that the Fourteenth Amendment *did* protect a person's economic rights. He found this meaning in the words "nor shall any State deprive any person of life, liberty, or property." One important economic right is the right to work. For this reason, any law that prevents a person from working violates his or her Fourteenth Amendment rights.

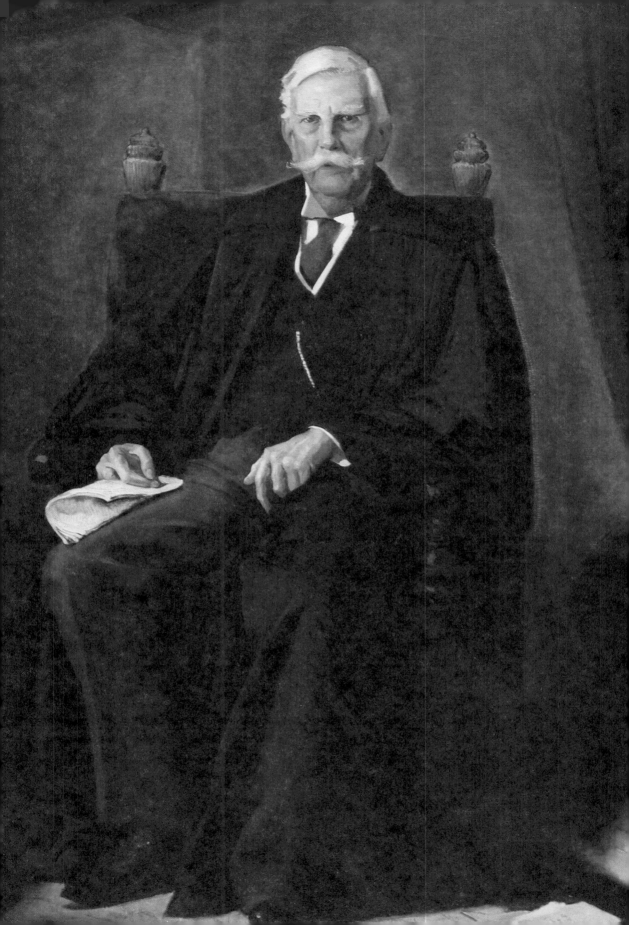

CHAPTER 5

The Shrinking of Congressional and State Power

"nor shall any State deprive any person of life, liberty, or property, without due process of law."

From the Fourteenth Amendment, 1868

An American who had spent some time out of the country during the Civil War years (1861 to 1865) would have come home to discover amazing changes. Not long before, the country's main industry had been farming. Most of the nation's businesspeople had been farmers. Now railroads and a variety of other businesses were springing up across the nation. Life in the United States would never be the same.

American citizens were becoming modern consumers who depended more and more upon the goods and services produced by others. The big national issues were changing, too. The old question of federal versus, or against, state power was being overshadowed—at least for the time being. This was the new question: Should the government control industry's appetites for profit, or should industry be free to do what it liked? The growth of private enterprise—privately owned businesses—certainly seemed to be a healthy development. Yet what was there to keep consumers and workers from being taken advantage of?

Oliver Wendell Holmes served on the Supreme Court from 1902 to 1932. He dissented from the majority decision in the *Lochner* case (1905). That Court decision held that individuals had economic rights (such as freedom of contract) that could not be interfered with by state law.

regulate railroads. Congress passed the Sherman Antitrust Act in 1890. Its purpose was to "protect trade and commerce against unlawful restraints [limits] and monopolies." (Trusts are corporations that join together to control prices and other policies.)

Legislation passed during the late nineteenth century dealt with business practices. But later regulations had to do with articles of commerce. This type of legislation focused on such things as a product's poor quality or its unhealthy or immoral nature. Between 1906 and 1916, Congress based various laws on the commerce and

The Meat Inspection Act of 1906 provided for federal inspection of all companies selling meat in interstate commerce. It also provided for the enforcement of sanitary rules in meat-packing businesses.

taxing powers. For instance, the Pure Food and Drug Act of 1906 outlawed impure foods or foods that were mismarked, if these foods had to do with interstate commerce. The Meat Inspection Act of 1906 ordered local inspection of meat and barred uninspected or bad meat from interstate commerce. The Mann Act of 1910 struck out at prostitution. It did so by outlawing the transportation of women across state lines for immoral purposes. In 1916 the first U.S. law that aimed to prevent the use of child labor was passed. These measures did not discourage the Supreme Court. It continued to support free enterprise.

In 1895 the Supreme Court heard the case of *United States* v. *E. C. Knight Co.* The federal government claimed that E. C. Knight—a powerful sugar company—had signed contracts with other, smaller companies. These agreements would make it possible for E. C. Knight to control more than 90 percent of all refined sugar in the United States. This, said the government, was an unfair business activity. It prevented other sugar companies in other states from doing business. The government wanted the Court to put E. C. Knight out of business. But the Court rejected the government's claim. It admitted that E. C. Knight did have control over the manufacture of sugar. But it said this control was *not* over interstate commerce. For this reason, said the Court, E. C. Knight's control wasn't illegal. The Court ruled that the Sherman Antitrust Act could not forbid monopolies having to do with manufacturing. If the federal government were given such authority, it would be invading the reserved powers of the state.

This and other judicial rulings successfully dealt both the Sherman Antitrust Act and the Interstate Commerce Commission serious blows.

In its various rulings, the Supreme Court had used the commerce clause to uphold the interests of private industry. Gradually, though, the Court had to turn to other parts of the Constitution for legal help. It soon became obvious that certain business practices *did* violate the laws of interstate commerce.

But Holmes's opinion was a minority opinion. Under the majority's Lochner doctrine, the Court declared many state laws invalid. (The record shows that more than 180 such decisions were handed down between 1899 and 1937. Most of these rulings were made from 1920 onward.) Some of these were based on the Fourteenth Amendment's due process clause. Others were based on the amendment's equal protection clause. Among the state regulations that the Court overturned were laws forbidding "yellow-dog" contracts (under which workers promised their bosses that they would not join a labor union). The Court also rejected laws that set minimum wages for women.

State Police Power Cases

One landmark case suggests how strongly the Supreme Court felt about government regulation. In 1916 Congress had passed a law forbidding goods made by children from being carried in interstate commerce. In 1918, in the case of *Hammer* v. *Dagenhart,* the Supreme Court declared this law unconstitutional. Justice William Day explained that this law was different from others the Court might have approved in the past. Those earlier laws blocked the movement of such things as impure food, which were *in themselves* actually harmful. The same could not be said of the goods in the *Dagenhart* case. This part of the Court's argument was not taken very seriously by the legal community.

But another part of the Court's opinion was more important. The Court held that in this case the federal law really had less to do with commerce than with regulating child labor. Pointing to the case of *United States* v. *E. C. Knight* (1895), Day said that conditions of labor were part of manufacturing, not commerce. As such, they came under state law. For this reason, the Court said, the federal law in question was unconstitutional. Why? Because it invaded the state's police power under the Tenth Amendment. Several times during the next twenty years, the Court decided that

Child labor in 1911. The Supreme Court in *Hammer* v. *Dagenhart* (1918) declared unconstitutional a federal law that had prohibited the shipment of goods made in factories employing children.

the powers reserved to the states (that is, powers to protect citizens' health, safety, welfare, and morals) were being invaded by a federal law.

CHAPTER 6

A New Deal for Everyone

"The powers not delegated to the United States by the Constitution . . ."

The Tenth Amendment, 1791

On October 24, 1929, the stock market crashed, and millions of Americans everywhere were sent sprawling. The Great Depression had begun. Production quickly dropped to half its normal level, and more than 12 million people found themselves out of work. President Herbert Hoover tried various remedies, but all his efforts failed. When Franklin D. Roosevelt became president in 1933, the country found its architect for change.

The New Deal Begins

During Roosevelt's first hundred days in office, he suggested scores of programs to help end the economic crisis. Congress passed most of them under its taxing and interstate commerce powers. Among the New Deal measures set up by Congress and President Roosevelt were the National Labor Relations Act, the National Bituminous Coal Conservation Act, the National Industrial Recovery Act, and the Agricultural Adjustment Act.

Unemployed workers line up for free food and lodging during the Great Depression. During the 1930s the federal government took an active role in enacting laws designed to help people and businesses. In the mid-1930s, the Court declared some of these laws unconstitutional.

and struck down eight New Deal programs. Among these were a section of the National Industrial Recovery Act, the NRA itself, the Railroad Retirement Pension Act, the Agricultural Adjustment Act, and the Bituminous Coal Act. Behind these rulings loomed the Tenth Amendment. Some scholars say that the Court twisted the amendment's meaning. That is, instead of forbidding the federal government to exercise powers not delegated to it, the amendment seemed to limit those delegated powers themselves. But it is also commonly held that Congress and President Roosevelt may have overstepped their constitutional limits.

In 1935 the Supreme Court ruled on the section of the NIRA that had been called into question. The case concerned oil. According to the NIRA, the president could forbid interstate shipping of oil beyond the limits allowed by the states. The purpose of this section of the law was to keep oil prices steady and save oil resources. In the case of *Panama Refining Co.* v. *Ryan* (1935), this section of the law was declared unconstitutional. The Court ruled that the law did not give the president enough guidelines.

In *Retirement Board* v. *Alton Railroad Co.* (1935), the Supreme Court canceled the Railroad Retirement Pension Act. The Court held that the details of the law violated due process and the Fifth Amendment. The Court also put forth the opinion that old-age pensions, or payments, had nothing to do with either the safety or the smooth running of railroad transportation. For this reason, the Court reasoned, the law had no real bearing on federal commerce.

The ruling in the *Schechter Poultry* (the "Sick Chicken") case hurt the NRA. Officially called *Schechter Poultry Corp.* v. *United States,* the case reached the Supreme Court in 1935. Two brothers named Schechter objected to the charge that they were breaking the poultry industry's code by selling sick chickens. The plaintiffs claimed that the government had no right to meddle with local commerce. The Court supported their claim. In a unanimous vote, it found the NIRA to be unconstitutional. Chief Justice Hughes observed that "extraordinary conditions [the hardships of the Great

Farm workers. The blue eagle of the NRA was the symbol used by businesses following the regulations of the National Industrial Recovery Act. The Supreme Court declared that law unconstitutional in 1935.

Depression] do not create or enlarge constitutional power.'' Congress, said the Court, should not have delegated its lawmaking power to private companies. Business groups should not have been given such sweeping powers to decide what laws should apply to particular industries. The Court's objections didn't stop there, however. In the opinion of the Court, the poultry code, by trying to regulate intrastate commerce (commerce within a state), had gone beyond the commerce power of the federal government.

the interstate shipment of factory goods made by young children). The period sometimes referred to as "big government," which had begun during the 1930s, continued.

Incorporation of the Bill of Rights

Ask a student of American history to identify the outstanding events of the 1920s and 1930s. What is he or she most likely to name? The Great Depression and the New Deal. These were, indeed, the events that drew the almost undivided attention of millions of Americans. But there was another major development taking place of which most Americans were unaware. This involved the states and the individual citizens. The Supreme Court was beginning to hear cases that focused on individual rights and state governments. More and more, the Supreme Court was deciding in favor of individual civil liberties.

Only four years before the 1929 stock market crash and the beginning of the Great Depression, an important case came before the Supreme Court. Benjamin Gitlow was a man who supported extreme left-wing causes. In 1925 Gitlow was convicted of having violated a New York State law. He was convicted of having "advocated [called for], advised, and taught the duty, necessity, and propriety [rightness] of overthrowing and overturning organized government by force, violence, and unlawful means by certain writings." Gitlow appealed to the Supreme Court. He said that the state law he was accused of breaking violated the Fourteenth Amendment's due process clause. In addition, he claimed that it violated the First Amendment's guarantee of freedom of speech. Gitlow lost his appeal. But Justice Edward C. Sanford made legal history in *Gitlow* v. *New York* (1925) by declaring the following:

> For present purposes we may and do assume that freedom of speech and of the press—which are protected by the First Amendment from abridgement—are among the fundamental personal rights and "liberties" protected by the due process clause of the Fourteenth Amendment from impairment [damage] by the States.

Sanford and the Court had officially stated that the Fourteenth Amendment protects individual liberties from state interference.

It didn't take long for several more cases concerning individual civil liberties and state laws to go before the Supreme Court. Incorporation really began to take hold. (As previously mentioned, incorporation is the process of making Bill of Rights protections apply to the states so that people are safeguarded against state actions that violate these rights.)

Fiske v. *Kansas* (1927) marked the first time an individual civil-liberty claim was upheld under the Fourteenth Amendment. The specific issue in this case was freedom of speech. *Stromberg* v. *California* (1931) was perhaps an even more important "free speech" case. The individual who brought suit was Yetta Stromberg, a nineteen-year-old member of the Young Communist League. At summer camp she had encouraged a group of young people to pledge allegiance to a red (Communist) flag. In so doing, Stromberg had violated a California law against displaying such flags. The Court upheld the plaintiff's First Amendment right of free speech, a right applied to protection against state action by the Fourteenth Amendment.

In *Near* v. *Minnesota* (1931), the Court again ruled to uphold a First Amendment right claimed under the Fourteenth Amendment. Chief Justice Hughes declared that a law that prevented certain material from being published violated "the liberty of the press guaranteed by the Fourteenth Amendment." He also stated that it "is no longer open to doubt that the liberty of the press and of speech is safeguarded by the due process clause of the Fourteenth Amendment from invasion by state action."

The Court then turned its attention to the case of *Powell* v. *Alabama* (1932). This case involved seven young black men who had been falsely accused of raping two white girls. The men were given only a one-day trial without proper legal advice. They were then convicted. The Supreme Court overturned this verdict. In the Court's opinion, Alabama had violated the men's Sixth Amendment rights. The Sixth Amendment guarantees the right to a fair trial. It also protects an individual's right to legal advice in capital criminal cases. Capital crimes are serious crimes that could lead to the death penalty.

De Jonge v. *Oregon* (1937) concerned the First Amendment right of freedom of assembly and the right to petition the government "for a redress of grievances." Dirk De Jonge had been convicted of taking part in a political meeting of the Communist party. The meeting had been a peaceful one. Chief Justice Hughes read the Court's opinion. He explained that "a peaceable assembly for lawful discussion, however unpopular the sponsorship [organizing group] cannot be made a crime." He also said that assembly is one of "those fundamental principles of liberty and justice" that apply to the states through the Fourteenth Amendment.

Another case, *Palko* v. *Connecticut* (1937), is like *Gitlow* v. *New York* (1925) in two important ways. First, both plaintiffs lost their appeals. Second, both cases were milestones, though each in a different way. Connecticut had charged Frank Palko with the murder of two policemen. Because of certain details, after Palko's first trial the state scheduled a second trial. Palko tried to block the second trial. He claimed that this would place him in jeopardy [danger] twice for the same crime. "Double jeopardy" is forbidden both by the Fifth Amendment and by the due process clause of the Fourteenth Amendment. However, Palko's objections were cast aside. He was convicted of first-degree murder. Palko then brought his case to the Supreme Court and again lost. But Justice Benjamin Cardozo's opinion in the case became a yardstick for measuring other individual-liberty cases.

In his opinion, Cardozo did not recommend that the entire Bill of Rights be incorporated. Instead, he established an "honor roll of superior rights." He also said that there were "fundamental principles of liberty and justice which lie at the base of our civil and political institutions." The most basic of these were the rights of freedom of thought and speech.

Although Cardozo looked only at certain individual rights, he did give a broad warning: The states would still be subject to the legal test of whether a challenged law went against the due process clause of the Fourteenth Amendment. This would not always be easy to decide. But there were two Supreme Court justices who had their own test of this. Justice Frankfurter said that such a violation must "shock the conscience." Justice Holmes, more direct, always asked of a possible civil-liberties violation, "Does it make you vomit?"

The Tenth Amendment is concerned with the powers of the federal government, the states, and the people. These three sources of power are always changing in relation to each other. But these changes were especially obvious during certain periods in the nation's history. The years from 1925 through the New Deal's 1930s were such years. Taking a backward glance at 1940, the shifting balance of powers is clear. The federal government had become much stronger than it had ever been. The people, too, were gaining considerable power. Under the Bill of Rights, their civil liberties were being protected more and more against abuses by the states. In fact, the only group to lose power were the supporters of states' rights.

Shifting Powers and Emerging Rights

"nor deny to any person within its jurisdiction the equal protection of the laws."

From the Fourteenth Amendment, 1868

Does the Constitution give Congress the right to use its delegated powers when they touch an area that has been reserved to the states? John Marshall thought so. This was his philosophy of national supremacy. Marshall was no supporter of states' rights. He believed that the power the Constitution gave to the federal government was much greater than the power it gave to the states.

But the Supreme Court certainly did not always share Marshall's philosophy. The landmark decision in *Hammer* v. *Dagenhart* (1918) was a famous example of this. The federal government had outlawed the shipping across state lines of products that were made by child labor. But, instead of taking the federal government's side, the Supreme Court in *Hammer* v. *Dagenhart* had upheld a business's right to use child labor. The Court explained that the federal commerce power *did* include stopping harmful goods from being sent across state lines. However, said the Court, this power did *not* include stopping the shipping of goods just because they had been

---

William H. Rehnquist has served on the Supreme Court since 1972 and has been the chief justice since 1986. In 1976 he presented the majority opinion in *National League of Cities* v. *Usery.* The Supreme Court declared that the Tenth Amendment prevents Congress from interfering with states' wage and hour laws for state employees.

made by children. The *Hammer* v. *Dagenhart* ruling gave a narrow meaning to the national commerce power. The guidelines set by this case were not officially rejected until 1941.

Social Welfare Regulation

Even before 1941, the Supreme Court had begun to support programs that helped the general public. (These kinds of programs are called social welfare programs.) The office of the presidency had also grown stronger. For these reasons, by 1940 the federal government had become much more powerful than the states. But the ruling handed down in *Hammer* v. *Dagenhart* (1918) still stood. Then, in 1941, the U.S. Supreme Court heard the case of *United States* v. *Darby*.

The case of *United States* v. *Darby* had to do with federal efforts to see that sections of the Fair Labor Standards Act of 1938 were obeyed. The Fair Labor Standards Act applied to all employees and employers who were directly involved in interstate commerce. It also affected workers who made products for interstate commerce. The Fair Labor Standards Act (FLSA) was made up of several sections. One part set a minimum wage of twenty-five cents an hour. In addition, it established that forty-four hours was the most hours a person could work without being paid extra money. Another part of the FLSA outlawed shipping products across state lines if they had been made by workers who were underpaid. The act also forbade the interstate shipping of goods made by any business that had used child labor within thirty days.

In *United States* v. *Darby* (1941) the Supreme Court unanimously upheld the Fair Labor Standards Act. In making its decision, the Court held that an operation in the lumber industry had to meet certain standards of child labor. In coming to this decision, the Court firmly supported the position that the Fair Labor Standards Act was constitutional. More important, however, it gave broad meaning to the commerce power. What the Court really said was that the federal government had the constitutional right to protect children as well as goods. In giving the majority opinion, Justice Harlan F. Stone said:

> Congress, following its own [idea] . . . concerning [limits] which may be imposed on interstate commerce, is free to exclude . . . those [goods] whose use in the states for which they are destined [meant] . . . may be [harmful] to the public health, morals, or welfare. . . . Our conclusion is unaffected by the Tenth Amendment. The Amendment states but a truism [an obvious truth] that all is retained which has not been surrendered.

In its *Darby* decision, the Court was also rejecting dual federalism. The Court showed that it did not go along with the idea that the federal and state governments have separate but equal areas of power. *Darby* began a period of national supremacy that lasted for more than thirty-five years. Congress was now free to use the commerce power for social welfare purposes. A brief discussion of a few Supreme Court decisions will illustrate this.

In 1946 the Court ruled against a state officer who sold timber on school lands. The officer's price had been above the limit set by the Office of Price Administration.

In 1954 the Court upheld a law that reduced federal aid for highway construction. (The federal government decided to give the state less money because the state had not fired a member of the highway commission who had broken a federal law.)

In 1968, in *Maryland* v. *Wirtz,* the Court made a decision in favor of extending the Fair Labor Standards Act. (The act now included laws about wages and hours for employees in state schools and hospitals.)

The Pendulum Swings

For thirty-five years, the Supreme Court's decisions helped federal lawmakers. Many rulings supported social welfare rather than private business interests. Then, in 1976, the Supreme Court did something startling. For the first time in forty years, it overturned a congressional law based on the commerce clause. The Court's decision in *National League of Cities* v. *Usery* struck like a thunderbolt.

Like *Maryland* v. *Wirtz* (1968), *Usery* concerned the Fair Labor Standards Act. Two years before *Usery,* in 1974, Congress had again added more parts to the act. As a result, federal minimum wages and maximum hours now covered almost *all* state and local government employees. While the Court had approved the earlier changes in *Maryland* v. *Wirtz,* in *National League of Cities* v. *Usery* (1976) it decided that the new changes were unconstitutional.

Justice William H. Rehnquist gave the majority opinion. He pointed out that the original Fair Labor Standards Act of 1938 did not apply to the states. It allowed the *federal government* to make wage and hour legislation for *private* employers under the commerce power. However, making laws telling the states what wages and hours to set for state employees violated the states' constitutional rights.

The [Tenth] Amendment expressly declares the constitutional policy that Congress may not exercise power in a fashion that impairs [harms] the States' integrity [soundness] or their ability to function effectively in a federal system.

According to the Supreme Court, Congress was not only interfering with the states' police power but also regulating the states as states. Rehnquist explained:

[T]he State might wish to employ persons with little or no training ... and pay them less than the federally prescribed [required] minimum wage.... It may wish to offer part-time or summer employment to teenagers at a figure less than the minimum wage, and if unable to do so may decline to offer such employment at all. But the Act would forbid such choices by the States.

Another justice, Lewis F. Powell, Jr., firmly believed that congressional action of this sort was a violation of the Tenth Amendment. Powell said that Congress had no more right to set employment rules for mass-transit workers than for those in police work, fire prevention, sanitation, or public health.

Justice William Brennan, on the other hand, was one of three dissenting justices. He argued:

> The only analysis even remotely resembling that adopted today is found in . . . opinions dealing with the Commerce Clause and the Tenth Amendment that . . . provoked a constitutional crisis for the Court in the 1930's. . . . It bears repeating "that effective restraints on . . . exercise [of the commerce power] must proceed from political rather than judicial processes." (*Wickard* v. *Filburn,* 1942)

For almost ten years, the Supreme Court lived with the 1976 *Usery* decision. The decision prevented the federal government from doing anything that would hurt the states' ability to carry out their "traditional functions." The Court struggled again and again with the question of Tenth Amendment limits on federal lawmaking powers. However, in cases where the national interest was involved, the Court often supported the federal government. Three cases are examples of this.

In *Hodel* v. *Virginia Surface Mining and Reclamation Association, Inc.* (1981), the Supreme Court upheld a law that set standards for surface coal mining. In *FERC* v. *Mississippi* (1982), the Court upheld federal legislation that forced state governments to study federal standards for saving energy. In *EEOC* v. *Wyoming* (1983), the Court upheld the Age Discrimination in Employment Act. Here it overturned a state policy that forced state game wardens to retire at age fifty-five.

The Pendulum Swings Back

It was Justice Harry A. Blackmun's vote that decided the *Usery* case. His vote also helped to overturn that decision nine years later. The case was *Garcia* v. *San Antonio Metropolitan Transit Authority* (1985). The issue in *Garcia* was once again the Fair Labor Standards Act. This time the question for the Supreme Court was whether laws about wages and hours applied to the employees of a city-owned mass-transit system. The Supreme Court had to ask itself, Is such ownership and operation a "traditional [state] governmental function?" The Supreme Court went further than this. It upheld federal law.

In upholding federal law, the Court explained that it was hard to tell the difference between "traditional governmental functions" and those that are not. For example, federal courts of appeal had held that the licensing of automobile drivers was a state function. Therefore, the federal government shouldn't interfere. However, the control of traffic on public roads was not a traditional function. Here, the Court said, the federal government had a right to exercise control.

The most important idea to come out of the *Garcia* decision was this: As long as Congress's use of the commerce power is constitutional, Congress may regulate states as well as private individuals. What follows from this idea? States should not generally expect the Supreme Court to set limits on federal control. Instead, the states will find their interests protected in the government systems that have already been set up to control Congress.

Justice Powell wrote an important dissenting opinion in *Garcia*. He expressed his concern that the majority opinion of the Court might give the federal government too much power. The result would be that "federal political officials, invoking [getting support from] the Commerce Clause, are the sole judges of the limits of their own power." He said that this contradicted the famous *Marbury* v. *Madison* decision (1803). In that case it was decided that the federal courts—not politicians—should "say what the law is.'' That is, the courts should decide whether laws passed by Congress are constitutional.

Justice Sandra Day O'Connor was also opposed to the majority opinion in the *Garcia* case. She gave a separate dissenting opinion. In it she observed that federal control was stronger than ever. Justice O'Connor believed that recent changes in how Congress worked "lessened the weight Congress gives to the legitimate interests of States as States.''

Was Justice O'Connor right to be afraid? The question is still being argued today. In any case, with the *Garcia* ruling, Congress regained its full commerce powers. This made it harder for a state to stop Congress from regulating state lawmaking processes. The federal government was again firmly buckled into the driver's seat.

The Civil Rights Movement

"Our Constitution is color-blind." Justice John M. Harlan gave this minority opinion in 1896. What did he mean by this? For one thing, Harlan meant that the states would have to be stopped from discriminating against, or being unfair to, people because of their race. He also meant that private discrimination against African Americans would have to end. Yet words are not deeds. In 1896 Harlan's statement was a dissent of one against a majority decision. For more than half a century, there was little change.

Justice Harlan had given his opinion in the famous case of *Plessy* v. *Ferguson*. Louisiana had passed a law in 1890 to keep African Americans separate from white people while traveling in railroad cars. This was one of several laws Southern states had passed to segregate, or separate, the races, in such public places as railroad trains, public parks, and hospitals. The Supreme Court case arose after Plessy, an African American, refused to leave a railroad car that was reserved for whites. Plessy was arrested, but he appealed his case until it reached the Supreme Court. The Court ruled that it was legal to have "separate but equal" facilities for "the white and colored races." This decision seemed to cripple any chances to end racial segregation. Many decades later, the words "separate but equal" were still being used to refer to and support racial segregation in the United States.

During these bleak years, the federal government did take a few steps to stop discrimination. For example, in 1941 the Interstate Commerce Commission (ICC) fought segregated trains. In the case of *Mitchell* v. *United States,* the Supreme Court held that African Americans could not be kept out of certain railroad cars. In *Henderson* v. *United States* (1950), the Court made a similar ruling concerning railroad sleeping cars and dining cars. In 1955 the ICC ordered an end to all racial segregation of trains and buses that crossed state lines. As the basis for its actions, the ICC used the commerce power. In spite of these efforts, segregation could be seen in every part of Southern society. (Segregation also existed in the North, but it was less obvious there.) Yet, as early as 1946, the seeds were being sown for much greater struggle and change. In that year President Harry S. Truman set up a Civil Rights Commission. The commission recommended laws against lynching and police cruelty toward African Americans. It suggested laws for equal voting. It also called for federal action to end segregation.

In 1948 something important happened at a national political convention. The members of the Democratic party decided to follow the suggestions of the Civil Rights Commission. They agreed to put a strong plan into action. This news angered delegates from Mississippi and Alabama. Waving the Confederate flag, these Southern delegates stormed out. Five days later, they formed the States' Rights party. Members of this party were known as the Dixiecrats.

As the civil rights movement grew stronger, so did states' rights groups. Supporters of segregation fought desegregation—which means doing away with laws and practices that separate people of different races—every step of the way. But the civil rights movement could not be stopped. It found a powerful friend in Chief

Justice Earl Warren. The Warren Court's decision was made in 1954. The case was *Brown* v. *Board of Education of Topeka.*

Brown v. *Board of Education of Topeka*

At that time in Topeka, Kansas, every public school was segregated. As in so many segregated situations, the claims were made that the schools for whites and those for blacks were "separate but equal." All the same, Linda Brown's parents wanted her to go to the white school just five blocks from their home. Instead, Linda had to travel twenty-one blocks to attend the nearest all-black school. The Browns decided to try to change things. They sued the Topeka Board of Education. The case ended up in the Supreme Court. The Supreme Court's decision in *Brown I* was unanimous: "Separate educational facilities are inherently [by their very nature] unequal." School segregation was therefore held to be unconstitutional. It violated the equal protection clause of the Fourteenth Amendment. In making this ruling, the Court had at last overthrown the earlier 1896 *Plessy* v. *Ferguson* decision. The lawyer who led the legal team on this case was Thurgood Marshall. Marshall later became the first African-American justice to serve on the Supreme Court.

Brown II (1955) dealt with correcting the wrongs caused by segregation. The Court ordered desegregation to begin "with all deliberate speed." This meant that changes had to be made as quickly as possible. But most Southern states fought these decisions as hard as they could. They tried to stop the Court from ruling on civil rights cases. They delayed. They even passed laws to avoid having to obey the federal government. Try as they might, though, they could not turn back the clock.

In one case after another, the federal government attacked racial segregation in public swimming pools, in parks, in theaters, and in other public places. In these cases, federal decisions were usually upheld. For example, in *Gayle* v. *Browder* (1956), the Court applied the desegregation ruling to city-run buses in Montgomery, Alabama.

The Supreme Court Expands the Meaning of State Action

Desegregation worked partly because of the expansion of the idea of state action. Remember, state action refers to the conduct of a state government or any of its subdivisions. These include cities, counties, city-owned companies such as bus companies, and so forth. According to the Supreme Court's *Civil Rights* cases decision in 1883, civil rights are protected against abuses by state governments and their subdivisions. But civil rights are not protected against private abuses. During the early 1940s, the Court began to broaden the idea of state action.

The Court began to rule that some actions of private individuals or groups that had violated civil rights could be connected to state action. In some cases, the Court ruled that actions by private individuals or groups were really actions performing a "public function." For example, private political parties could not discriminate in some of their practices, such as choosing their own candidates in primaries. The reason given was that the whole election process was a public function even if the political parties were private.

Another way in which the Court began to broaden its idea of state action was to look closely not at the action of the private individual but at the conduct of the state. If the state government seemed involved with or encouraged or benefited from a private individual's or group's actions, then state action could be claimed. For example, this might happen if a state enforced a private agreement between a home seller and a home buyer that the house only be owned by other white people for the next fifty years.

The expansion of state action to apply to cases of racial discrimination reached its peak during the 1960s, when Earl Warren was chief justice of the United States.

Civil Disobedience

African-American leaders and their supporters also tried to end segregation in privately owned businesses. They did this by taking part in civil disobedience. Civil disobedience takes place when people refuse to obey certain laws. People take part in civil disobedience because they hope to change these laws. One example

Sit-ins were held throughout the South in order to integrate lunch counters and other public facilities. Those who opposed integration often used harassment or violence to try to preserve segregation of the races.

of civil disobedience would be not paying taxes that are being spent on war.

In the civil rights movement, an example of civil disobedience was the sit-in. During a sit-in, a group of African Americans would go into a segregated restaurant, sit down in the "whites only" section, and demand to be served. Of course, in doing this they were breaking state or local segregation laws. When the group was asked to leave, they continued "sitting in." This often led to their arrest and conviction. That in turn brought segregation laws to the attention of many other people. Sit-ins also announced that African Americans would no longer accept these laws.

New Civil Rights Laws

During the early 1960s, sit-ins against private businesses were hard for the Supreme Court to defend. But in 1964 Congress passed a new civil rights act. The Civil Rights Act of 1964 covered many areas. One part of the act protected voting rights. Another section dealt with public accommodation. It said that everyone should have "the full and equal enjoyment" of public places. This included privately owned hotels, motels, restaurants, motion-picture houses, theaters, concert halls, and sports arenas. These guarantees applied to any place if it "affects commerce" or if discrimination was supported by state action. A third section of the act guaranteed African Americans entrance to public parks, stadiums, and swimming pools. A fourth section stated that the federal government would give money to all schools that were trying to desegregate. Yet another section stated that federal money could not go to operate educational programs that practiced discrimination.

In 1964 a new amendment was added to the Constitution. The Twenty-fourth Amendment was created to do away with state laws that demanded that people pay a tax before they could vote.

Then, in 1965, the Voting Rights Act was passed to make sure that African Americans were actually allowed to vote. This act did away with literacy (reading) tests and other efforts to prevent African Americans from voting. It also called for federal workers to go into states where the law was disobeyed. These workers then helped African Americans to register and vote.

In 1968 another civil rights act was passed. The most important part of this law had to do with open housing. It stated that owners could not refuse to sell or rent houses because of someone's race, color, or place of birth.

States' rights supporters hated many of these laws and the rulings of the Supreme Court that supported these laws. They claimed that these rulings weakened state powers. The federal government had no right to interfere with segregation, said the states' rights people. This kind of interference violated the police power of the states.

The idea that every state has the right of interposition came to life once more. (This was John Calhoun's belief more than 100 years earlier.) As was discussed in Chapter 3, interposition means that a state has the right to interpose, or put, the state's power against any federal power that interfered with it. In other words, a state may strike down federal decisions that contradict state laws. Segregationists now used this doctrine to defend their attempts to block desegregation.

Supporters of states' rights had a strong leader in George Wallace. As governor of Alabama during the 1960s, Wallace fought desegregation. In 1963 he unsuccessfully tried to stop several African Americans from enrolling at the University of Alabama. In 1968 Wallace wanted to run for president of the United States. When he couldn't get the support of the Democrats, he formed a third party. It was named the American Independent Party. This party was dedicated to upholding the principles of states' rights. In the 1968 presidential election, Wallace came in third, with 10 million votes.

In the meantime, the civil rights movement was growing stronger. Dr. Martin Luther King, Jr., had begun to attract national attention in his leadership of the movement. In 1955 and 1956, Dr. King led a bus boycott in Montgomery, Alabama. (To boycott is to refuse to use a service or buy a product. Boycotts are a way of applying economic pressure. If people withdraw their business, they can do powerful damage to a company's profits.) The boycott was organized because Montgomery's segregation laws forced African Americans to sit or stand in the back of buses. It went on for an entire year. So did the legal battle.

In the end, a federal court ruled that the laws that created segregated buses were unconstitutional. The case was then appealed to the Supreme Court, which, in 1956, affirmed—that is, agreed with—the lower federal court's ruling. Segregation on the city's buses was held to be unconstitutional. The boycotters had won. They had gotten what they wanted without using any violence. This form of fighting is called nonviolent resistance. Dr. King was a great believer in nonviolent resistance. Sit-ins and boycotts were used throughout the 1960s. Along with the legal battles, they resulted in the desegregation of lunch counters in stores all over the South. The public-accommodations provisions of the Civil Rights Act of 1964 added more muscle to the fight for equal rights. They were first tested in the case of *Heart of Atlanta* v. *United States* (1964). Heart of Atlanta was a Georgia motel that refused to serve African Americans. The Supreme Court held that Congress had the power to forbid racial discrimination in hotels and motels serving interstate travelers. Although the discrimination took place locally, it discouraged African Americans from traveling. The discrimination therefore affected interstate commerce.

Katzenbach v. *McClung* (1964) was a related case. It involved Ollie's Barbecue, a small, local restaurant in Birmingham, Alabama. In upholding the commerce power in this case, the Supreme Court used interesting reasoning. It was true, the Court said, that only 46 percent of Ollie's food came through interstate commerce. But the policy of not serving African Americans kept some of this food from being sold. Therefore, said the Court, interstate commerce was being blocked. The result was that business in general suffered. Because of this ruling, it can be said that the commerce power tipped the balance in the fight for equal rights. What made the civil rights movement a Tenth Amendment issue? It was part of the long and continuing struggle between the federal government and supporters of states' rights.

Further Incorporation of the Bill of Rights

Chief Justice Earl Warren served on the Supreme Court for fifteen years. He came to be seen as one of the strongest chief justices the Court ever had. One reason for this view was Warren's central role in helping African Americans gain their civil rights. But Warren did even more than this. During his last eight years on the bench, Warren helped to make sure that everyone's civil liberties were more carefully protected. The following cases are among the rulings that the Supreme Court handed down under Warren.

Mapp v. *Ohio* (1961) involved a woman named Dolree Mapp. The police had forcibly entered her home. They then searched it without a warrant. They found unlawful pornographic literature, and, for that, she was later convicted. Mapp fought her conviction. She claimed that the evidence had been taken illegally. After a state court upheld her conviction, the Supreme Court reversed that decision. The Court ruled that "all evidence obtained by searches and seizures in violation of the Constitution is, by that same authority [the Fourth Amendment of the Constitution] inadmissible [not permitted] in a state court."

Robinson v. *California* (1962) concerned the Eighth Amendment. (This amendment protects citizens from "cruel and unusual punishments.") Walter Robinson was arrested by the Los Angeles police after he told them he used drugs. The police also saw what might have been needle marks on Robinson's arm. Robinson's lawyer raised the "cruel and unusual punishments" issue. The lawyer said that the law did not have proof that Robinson had bought or used drugs. The Court declared the arrest unconstitutional. Justice Potter Stewart said that "a state which imprisons a person thus afflicted [stricken] as a criminal, even though he had never touched any narcotic drug within the state or been guilty of any irregular behavior there, inflicts a cruel and unusual punishment in violation of the Fourteenth Amendment."

Gideon v. *Wainwright* (1963) was an especially important case. Clarence Gideon had been sent to a Florida jail for "having broken and entered a poolroom with intent to commit a misdemeanor [minor crime]." The man whose testimony sent Gideon to jail later turned out to be the guilty party. At his trial, Gideon, who had no money, had been refused legal help. Florida law held that the court had to provide this kind of help only in capital cases—cases that might lead to the convicted person's execution. When the case came before the Supreme Court, Justice Hugo L. Black stated that it was an "obvious truth" that "in our... system of criminal justice any person hailed into court who is too poor to hire a lawyer cannot be assured a fair trial unless counsel [legal help] is provided for him." As a result of this case, a Sixth Amendment guarantee could not legally be abused by the states. Since then, legal counsel has been given in almost all criminal cases, even if that meant a court-appointed lawyer.

Griswold v. *Connecticut* (1965) concerns the right to privacy (a right that has been touched upon by various amendments). In this case the Court struck down a state law involving birth control. The Connecticut law had made it a crime for any person—married or single—to use any drug or object that prevented pregnancy. Justice William O. Douglas spoke for the Supreme Court in its 7-2 decision:

> Various guarantees create zones of privacy.... The Ninth Amendment provides: "the enumeration in the Constitution, of certain rights, shall not be construed [considered] to deny or disparage [make less important] others retained by the people."

The first nine amendments of the Bill of Rights relate to the Tenth Amendment in one particularly important way. All of the amendments give guarantees and protections. When these protections are applied to the federal government, they limit the power of that government. When these protections are applied to state governments, they limit the power of those governments. In both cases, it is the people who benefit.

CHAPTER 8

State Power, Individual Rights, and the Teenager

"Students . . . are possessed of fundamental rights which the State must respect, just as they themselves must respect their obligations to the State."

JUSTICE ABE FORTAS, in *Tinker* v. *Des Moines School District* (1969)

Anyone under the age of seventeen who plans to visit Mesquite, Texas, had better know about this law: "It shall be unlawful for any owner, operator or displayer of coin-operated amusement machines [such as electronic games] to allow any person under the age of seventeen (17) years to play or operate a coin-operated amusement machine unless such minor is accompanied by a parent or legal guardian."

Similar laws have been passed in a number of American cities. These laws are meant to protect young people. In this case, the lawmakers may have wanted to prevent from wasting time and money those people who might find it hard to stop. Are these laws constitutional? The final verdict is not in. The Mesquite law was brought before the Supreme Court. But the Court avoided ruling on its constitutionality. On the other hand, the law was declared unconstitutional by a lower federal court. That court found that the law limiting electronic games did not serve a good enough state purpose. In other words, it was outside of the police power of the state.

The national government's Fair Labor Standards Act has certain rules about what kinds of work teenagers can legally perform. States also have their own child labor laws.

What does all this mean? Are there many more state laws telling teenagers what they can do, and when? What about constitutional rights? Do any of the guarantees in the Bill of Rights apply to teenagers? The answer to these questions is *yes.*

State Laws and Young People

Every American citizen is limited by state laws. A state's police power is supposed to safeguard the health, safety, and welfare of all of its citizens. As part of this obligation, the state has the power to protect those who can't take complete care of themselves. Minors— young people who have not reached the age of majority—fall into this group. The age of majority is the age at which the law considers a person to be an adult. Each state decides its own age of majority. In most states it is eighteen.

Can states set a different age of majority for males and females? No. In fact, the Supreme Court ruled on this very question in 1975. A Utah law had set the age of majority for girls at eighteen and for boys at twenty-one. In *Stanton* v. *Stanton,* the Court ruled that it is unconstitutional to base the majority age on gender (sex). Doing so goes against the equal protection clause of the Fourteenth Amendment. The Court stated:

[N]o longer is the female destined solely for the home and the rearing of the family, and only the male for the marketplace and the world of ideas. . . . If a specified age of majority is required for the boy in order to assure him parental support while he obtains his education and training, so, too, it is for the girl.

Each state sets its own minimum, or lowest age limit, for certain activities. What are some activities for which the state sees the need to set the minimum age? Examples include attending school, getting a driver's license, voting in state elections, serving on a jury, marrying without parents' consent, receiving medical care without parents' consent, buying and drinking alcoholic beverages, and buying cigarettes.

States can set the minimum age for such activities as getting a driver's license, buying alcoholic drinks, and marrying.

What about a fifteen-year-old girl living in Bloomington, Indiana, who decides to buy a pack of cigarettes? Is she breaking the state law? No. In Indiana it is legal for a thirteen-year-old to buy cigarettes. Where can a young person legally leave school at age thirteen? In Mississippi. Which state requires someone to be sixteen and one month to get a driver's license? Again, Indiana.

Are states allowed by law to set different ages for males and females on any of these activities? So far, different states do have different age limits for each gender. For example, in Mississippi boys can get married at the age of fifteen without their parents' consent. Girls must be seventeen. Not long ago, the Supreme Court decided that states may not stop only males between certain ages from buying alcoholic beverages. (More recently, twenty-one became the legal age for everyone in every state.) As time goes on, there may be more such decisions. The key question seems to be: Are different limits for each gender necessary or are they based only on worn-out ideas about men and women?

Federal and State Laws That Protect Young People

Teenagers are understandably impatient in the face of so many limits on their behavior. But most laws are honestly meant to protect. One area in which both federal and local laws apply is that of child labor.

Child labor laws limit the kinds of jobs children can have. They also give the minimum age that a person must be in order to work, the maximum hours the person may work, and so on. Child labor laws in the United States began more than ninety years ago. At that time, children—even very young children—were used for cheap labor. They worked long hours for low pay under terrible conditions. The Fair Labor Standards Act of 1938 was passed to prevent just such abuses. Among other things, the law prohibited an employer from using child labor to make goods that were to be used in interstate commerce. Various Supreme Court rulings have since given *interstate commerce* a very broad meaning. For this reason, most American employers are covered by the Fair Labor Standards Act.

Under this act, most work is off limits to young people under age fourteen. Teenagers between fourteen and sixteen are allowed to work in certain "nonmanufacturing" jobs, but these jobs must not interfere with school. Young people under eighteen may not be hired for jobs that are dangerous. This means that a seventeen-year-old may scoop ice cream, but he may not operate a meat-slicing machine. A seventeen-and-a-half-year-old may not work on a wrecking crew, but she is allowed to be a camp counselor.

In addition to federal laws, every state has its own child labor laws. The laws are quite specific. For example, in Illinois, a teenager still under sixteen may not work in a bowling alley or a skating rink. In New York, a twelve year old may harvest berries, fruits, and vegetables. She may not, however, clean windows until she is eighteen. State employment offices have the exact child labor laws for their state. School guidance counselors may also provide booklets giving a state's child labor laws. There are many different ways in which states use their police powers to pass laws to protect young people. However, it soon becomes clear that lawmakers in the states have to think about more than the limits. They must also consider teenagers' constitutional rights.

Teenagers' Rights

When children become teenagers, what constitutional rights are theirs to enjoy? First Amendment rights to freedom of speech, expression, and thought. Fourth Amendment protections against unfair searches and seizures. Fifth Amendment guarantees that "no person . . . shall be compelled in any criminal case to be a witness against himself." Sixth Amendment guarantees of the right to legal advice. Fourteenth Amendment guarantees that no state shall "deprive any person of life, liberty, or property, without due process of law." And rights to privacy that are guaranteed by several of the amendments.

First Amendment Guarantees

In 1969 the Supreme Court handed down a landmark decision. The case was *Tinker* v. *Des Moines Independent Community School District.* The Supreme Court ruled that junior high and high school students "may express their opinions, even on controversial subjects."

The events that led to *Tinker* took place in 1965. While the war in Vietnam raged, some students and adults met in a home in Des Moines, Iowa. They had strong objections to the United States's participation in the Vietnam War. To show their feelings publicly, the students planned to wear black armbands to school. When the principals of the local schools heard of this plan, they acted immediately. Any student who wore an armband would be asked to take it off. If the student refused, he or she would be suspended. The student could return to school only without the armband.

When Mary Beth Tinker, John Tinker, and Christopher Eckhardt wore armbands to their schools, the expected happened. The three students were sent home and suspended from their junior high and high schools. But what happened next surprised the principals. The students' fathers filed a complaint with the courts. *Tinker* v. *Des Moines Independent Community School District* first went to lower courts, then reached the Supreme Court. In 1969 the Court ruled that wearing an armband to express one's views is protected by the free speech clause of the First Amendment. The Court's opinion states:

> Freedom of expression would not truly exist if the right could be exercised only in an area that a [kind] government provided as a safe haven for crackpots. . . . [W]e do not confine the . . . exercise of First Amendment rights to a telephone booth or the four corners of a pamphlet.

The Court ruled that students may be prevented from expressing their views *only if they disrupt the work and discipline of the school and interfere with the rights of other students.* The Court noted that the school district had been trying to avoid the controversy of antiwar feelings. The Court also pointed out that the school district had not banned other symbols that could be or were worn by students.

The Court's decision in the *Tinker* case extends to many activities that involve students' First Amendment rights. What are some of these activities? Wearing buttons that express strong opinions. Forming afterschool clubs whose members hold unpopular points of view. Handing out underground newspapers on school grounds. Being allowed to have and use school library books of which the officials may disapprove.

The Court has applied the *Tinker* principle to many of the issues raised by students' activities. One example is the *Island Trees* case (1982). A school board had ordered the removal of nine books from its school libraries. The books, claimed the board, went against the values of both the school board and the community. The Supreme

Court insisted that school officials "may not remove books from school library shelves simply because they dislike the ideas contained in those books." It held that a school library offers an "environment especially appropriate for the recognition of the First Amendment rights of students."

Fourth Amendment Guarantees

Under the Fourth Amendment, young people are protected against unreasonable searches. Searches are legal only under certain conditions. For instance, searches are legal with search warrants or if a person agrees to be searched. Young people are also protected against unreasonable seizures. This means that when evidence is taken as the result of an illegal search, it may not be used in Court. Students are also protected against unreasonable searches and seizures while they are in school. But in such cases the law is somewhat different. In *New Jersey* v. *T.L.O.* (1985), the Supreme Court laid out a few ground rules to guide school searches. A school official must have "reasonable grounds," or good reasons, for thinking the search will turn up some evidence. In addition, the search must be a limited one. States are free to set even stricter standards of protection than the federal government's.

Fifth and Sixth Amendment Guarantees

Before questioning a person—young or old—who has been arrested, in most states the police must read the Miranda warnings. These warnings are based on a case known as *Miranda* v. *Arizona* (1966). Miranda had been arrested for kidnapping and rape. He was taken to a special room for questioning. There, he signed a confession. The statement said he had confessed of his own free will. But he was not told that he could remain silent. Nor was he given the right to counsel.

The decision in *Miranda* established the Miranda warnings. They have been slightly changed to fit the needs of minors. The list of warnings varies. First, a person does not have to say anything except in answer to the request for name, age, address, and name of parents. Second, a person has the right to call parents, a lawyer, or both. Third, a person can stop answering questions at any time. Fourth, a person must be told that any questions he or she answers may be used against him or her in court.

In addition, the law goes to great trouble to protect the rights of minors in criminal cases. Confessions that are not freely given do not stand up in court.

Fourteenth Amendment Guarantees

How does "due process" apply to teenagers? Government agencies must treat all persons fairly. For instance, school officials cannot seriously punish a student for unacceptable behavior without first following certain steps. The case of *Goss* v. *Lopez* provided the guidelines that are now followed. In 1971 there was a great deal of student unrest in Columbus, Ohio. Nine high school students there were suspended without hearings for causing trouble. Some missed as many as ten days of school. *Goss* v. *Lopez* (1975) went before the Supreme Court. The Court held that "a 10-day suspension from school . . . may not be imposed in complete disregard of the Due Process Clause." Furthermore, the Court ruled that due process required that the suspended student be given "oral or written notice of the charges against him and, if he denies them, an explanation of the evidence the authorities have and an opportunity to present his side of the story."

Privacy Rights

The Bill of Rights never mentions the word *privacy*. But the Supreme Court has ruled that the different guarantees of the Bill of Rights create "zones of privacy." One of the most famous and debated privacy decisions ever made was handed down in 1973. In *Roe* v. *Wade,* the Court overturned Texas's antiabortion law. The ruling made abortion legal in every state. The Supreme Court ruled that states could not ban or even closely regulate abortions during the first three months of pregnancy. The choice of having an abortion during these months was left to the woman and her doctor. During the second three months, the states could regulate abortions to protect the woman's life or health. During the final three months, the states could regulate and even ban abortions except those necessary to preserve the life of the woman.

How does *Roe* v. *Wade* affect teenagers? Some sources say that more than 1 million teenage pregnancies take place each year. Of these, more than 80 percent are accidental. Most pregnant teenagers are unmarried. About 40 percent choose abortion. As of 1989, thirty-one states passed laws restricting a teenager's right to abortion. Some of the laws require teenagers under eighteen to either tell their parents or get their permission before having the abortion. Some states have passed these laws but have not enforced them. This is because the laws were ruled unconstitutional by either a state or a federal court. Eleven states do enforce these laws. Other states are thinking about passing new legislation.

What does an examination of state powers and teenagers' rights reveal? For one thing, states use their powers to control (and protect) many areas of teenagers' lives. In fact, the federal and state governments often work together for the protection of teenagers. In addition, teenagers have certain civil rights. Although the power of government in their lives is great, it is *not* unlimited. It is clear that the Tenth Amendment issue of state and national powers affects young people as well as adults. As teenagers approach the age of majority, their behavior becomes more like that of adults. As legal controls become fewer, constitutional rights increase. With these rights comes responsibility.

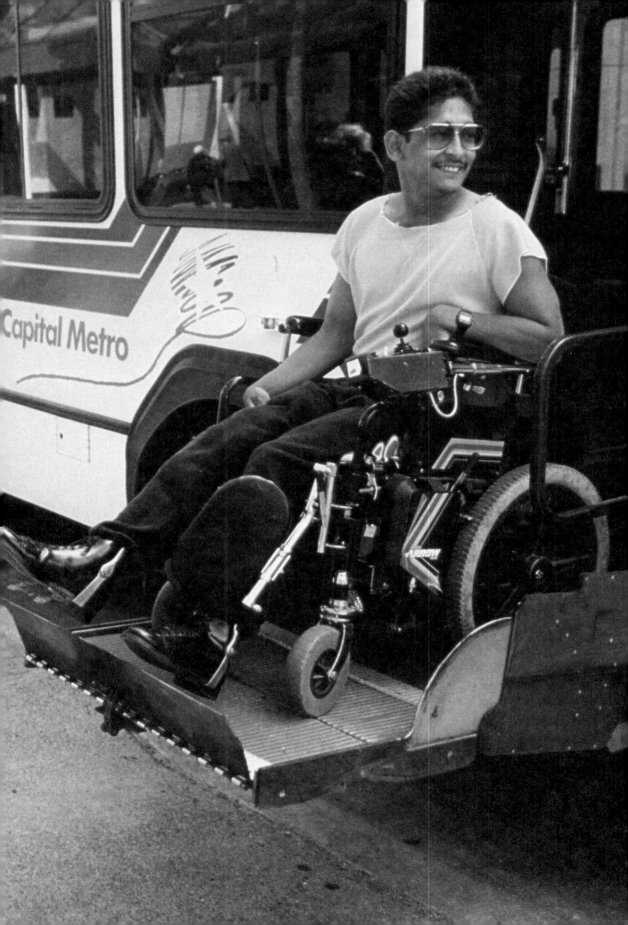

The Tenth Amendment Today

"The powers not delegated to the United States by the Constitution, nor prohibited by it to the States, are reserved to the States respectively."

From the Tenth Amendment, 1791

Is the federal government going too far in its use of power? Are the states free to use all their constitutional rights? Is the Tenth Amendment disappearing? The first two questions have been asked by lawmakers and others for more than 200 years. The third question is fairly new.

What does this third question suggest? Does it perhaps indicate that there is no longer any real doubt whether the federal government and the states are equally powerful? They are not. The federal government now plays an enormous role in the lives of Americans. Supreme Court decisions seem to support this fact. From 1964 to 1986, the Court declared forty-eight congressional acts to be unconstitutional. During the same period, it struck down 399 state or local acts.

In 1990 Congress passed and President George Bush signed the Americans with Disabilities Act. All except small businesses are required to hire and promote workers without regard to disabilities. Transportation systems are required to buy new vehicles that can be used by the disabled. Some felt that such regulations should be left to the states.

Recent Tenth Amendment Cases

One group of cases that took shape during the 1980s had to do with the federal government's commerce power. Until 1982 each state decided what size and weight tractor trailer trucks had to be. The federal government required only that the limits set be reasonable. The government did not want the vehicles to put any strain on interstate commerce. In 1982 the federal government passed the Surface Transportation Assistance Act (STAA). New federal regulations were passed that canceled the states' authority. Federal guidelines allowed certain tractor trailer trucks to be longer than they were before. The purpose of the act was to apply similar weight and length limits on all trucks that traveled on National Network highways (a national system of interstate and other highways). In doing this, the government hoped to ease the flow of interstate commerce. It also aimed to allow truckers to carry more products.

Truckers were happy with the STAA. The states, however, weren't. The states resented having one of their powers taken away. They also had practical objections. For instance, some people believed that massive trucks would damage the highways.

The Supreme Court heard several STAA cases during the 1980s. Among them were *United States* v. *Connecticut* (1983), *United States* v. *Florida* (1984), *National Freight, Inc.* v. *Larson* (1985), and *New York State Motor Truck Assoc.* v. *New York* (1987). The cases were not identical. Neither were the opinions of the Court. But, always, the Court upheld the STAA.

In 1988 a major tax case came before the Supreme Court. The case was *South Carolina* v. *Baker*. This dispute concerned a law that permitted the federal taxing of state and local bonds. When governments need money, one way of getting it is to borrow the money by selling bonds. Those who buy the bonds earn interest on them. The government that issues the bonds also promises to pay back to the lenders a certain sum of money on or before a specific date. For some time, states had a wonderful way to attract buyers for state and local bonds: These bonds were tax exempt. This meant that bond owners didn't have to pay federal taxes on the interest their bonds earned. Then a federal law removed the tax exemption from certain bonds. This was a bitter blow. It threatened to discourage buyers. Fewer buyers would mean reduced income for the states. Nevertheless, in *South Carolina* v. *Baker* (1988), the Supreme Court upheld the federal tax law.

In contrast, in *Garcia* v. *San Antonio Metropolitan Transit Authority* (1985), the Court had said:

> [O]ur examination . . . over the last eight years now persuades us that the attempts to draw the boundaries of state regulatory immunity [freedom from federal regulation] in terms of "traditional governmental function" is not only unworkable but [does not fit in] with established principles of federalism.

Some people believe that the issue behind *South Carolina* v. *Baker* was that the boundaries of state immunity were crossed in a dramatic way. John Sununu, President George Bush's White House chief of staff, made the following statement about these two cases:

> Two Supreme Court cases, Garcia vs. San Antonio Transit Authority (1985) and South Carolina vs. Baker (1988), have brought to a head concerns about the erosion of state authority. By making Congress the arbiter [judge] of its own actions, which affect the states, the two decisions not only weakened (some would say eliminated) 10th Amendment protection but also undercut the ability of states to attend to their responsibilities.

Current Trends

The Constitution was written in a simpler age. The Framers did not have the lenses through which to see even the dim outlines of modern American life. Some of the problems that were surely undreamed of in 1787 include crime and gun control, social welfare, civil rights, minority rights, rights for the disabled, environmental concerns, the right to life, and the right to die. Underlying all these issues are the old questions of powers and rights.

The federal government and the states have had a complicated relationship. It has always included both struggle and cooperation. The federal courts have commonly been considered the main guardians of individual rights. In fact, the Supreme Court has often protected the individual against abuses by the state. But this may now be changing. Today it is often the states that are the protectors of individual rights. The Supreme Court seems to be taking a narrow, more conservative point of view.

What happened not long ago in Minnesota is an example of a state court protecting individual rights. Members of the local Amish religious community there were in the habit of driving around very slowly in horse-drawn buggies. They refused to put triangular reflectors on their buggies as a safety measure. In 1989, when the police decided to give the Amish drivers traffic tickets, the drivers objected. They argued that their religion forbade them to put symbols such as triangles on their buggies. The case went before the state court. Although the court supported the First Amendment rights of the Amish, the matter did not end there. The case went before the U.S. Supreme Court. The Court ruled that states *could* indeed enforce laws that applied to everyone, and religious groups had to obey. Instead of dropping the issue, the Minnesota court decided that it didn't need to rely on the U.S. Constitution. Instead, it turned to its state constitution. There it found protection for religious freedom. The state court ruled that the reflector law violated the *state* constitutional rights of the Amish. The court firmly upheld these rights.

State courts have guarded individual liberties in cases involving free speech, abortion rights, freedom to follow sexual preference, and environmental issues. Nothing prevents the states from doing this. Every state *must* provide at least as much protection as the federal Constitution requires. But there is nothing to stop the states from providing even *more* protection than that.

So the struggle between federal and state power may have entered a new phase. It is too soon to say what the next chapter will be. But one thing is certain: The drama will continue.

$\mathscr{I}$MPORTANT $\mathscr{D}$ATES

1791 Tenth Amendment is approved by the states.

1803 *Marbury* v. *Madison.* Supreme Court declares that it has the power of judicial review and exercises it. This is the first case in which the Court holds a law of Congress to be unconstitutional.

1810 *Fletcher* v. *Peck.* Supreme Court refuses to uphold a state law that it considers unconstitutional.

1819 *McCullough* v. *Maryland.* Supreme Court upholds the implied right of the federal government to establish a national bank and denies states the right to tax the federal government.

1824 *Gibbons* v. *Ogden.* Supreme Court defines Congress's power to regulate commerce, including trade between states and within states if that commerce affects other states.

1833 *Barron* v. *Baltimore.* Supreme Court rules that the Bill of Rights applies only to actions of the federal government, not to the states and local governments.

1837 *Charles River Bridge* v. *Warren Bridge.* Supreme Court rules that a contract does not give implied rights that extend beyond the specific terms of the contract.

1851 *Cooley* v. *Board of Wardens of the Port of Philadelphia.* Supreme Court rules that states can apply their own rules to some foreign and interstate commerce if their rules are of a local nature—unless or until Congress makes rules for particular situations.

1857 *Dred Scott* v. *Sandford.* Supreme Court denies that African Americans are citizens even if they happen to live in a "free state."

1861 Eleven Southern states secede from the Union.

1861–65 Civil War

1868 Fourteenth Amendment is ratified. All people born or naturalized in the United States are citizens. Their privileges and immunities are protected, as are their life, liberty, and property according to due process. They have equal protection of the laws.

1873 *Slaughter-House* Cases. Supreme Court rules that the Fourteenth Amendment does not limit state power to make laws dealing with economic matters. Court mentions the unenumerated right to political participation.

1895 *United States* v. *E. C. Knight Co.* Supreme Court rules that a federal antitrust law does not apply to a monopoly in which the company is engaged in manufacturing, not commerce.

1903 *Champion* v. *Ames.* Supreme Court upholds federal law prohibiting the shipment of lottery tickets in interstate commerce.

1905 *Lochner* v. *New York.* Supreme Court strikes down a state law regulating maximum work hours.

1918 *Hammer* v. *Dagenhart.* Supreme Court declares unconstitutional a federal law prohibiting the shipment between states of goods made by young children.

1920 *Missouri* v. *Holland.* Supreme Court upholds the broad treaty-making power of the federal government and acknowledges its supremacy over state law.

1925 *Gitlow* v. *New York.* Supreme Court rules that freedom of speech is protected from state laws by the Fourteenth Amendment.

1935 *Schechter Poultry Corp.* v. *United States.* Supreme Court rules that Congress cannot delegate legislative power to the president in matters of trade and commerce. In regulating commerce within a state, the federal government exceeds its commerce power.

1936 *United States* v. *Butler.* Supreme Court strikes down a federal act requiring farmers to accept government payments in return for cutting down production of crops.

1937 Announcement of Roosevelt's court-packing bill. This measure, which never came to pass, could have increased the number of Supreme Court justices from nine to fifteen.

1941 *United States* v. *Darby.* Supreme Court upholds the prohibition of movement of certain goods in interstate commerce.

1954 *Brown* v. *Board of Education of Topeka.* Supreme Court holds that segregation on the basis of race (in public education) denies equal protection of the laws.

1964 *Heart of Atlanta* v. *United States.* Supreme Court upholds, as part of Congress's power under the commerce clause, its right to forbid racial discrimination in hotels and motels that serve interstate travelers.

1964 *Katzenbach* v. *McClung.* Supreme Court holds that Congress is exercising its commerce power in prohibiting racial discrimination in a restaurant that received much of its food from out of the state.

1973 *Roe* v. *Wade.* Supreme Court declares that the right to privacy protects a woman's right to end pregnancy by abortion under certain circumstances.

1976 *National League of Cities* v. *Usery.* Supreme Court holds that the Tenth Amendment prevents Congress from making federal minimum wages and overtime rules apply to state and city workers.

1981 *Hodel* v. *Virginia Surface Mining and Reclamation Association, Inc.* Supreme Court upholds the application of federal regulations to states involved in strip mining.

1982 *Federal Energy Regulation Commission* v. *Mississippi.* Supreme Court rules that state public utility commissions have to consider a set of federal proposals in order to continue regulating in that area.

1983 *Equal Employment Opportunity Commission* v. *Wyoming.* Supreme Court holds that a federal act regulating age discrimination in employment may be extended to state and local government employees.

1985 *Garcia* v. *San Antonio Metropolitan Transit Authority.* Supreme Court rules that Congress can make laws dealing with wages and hour rules applied to city-owned transportation systems.

1987 *New York State Motor Truck Association* v. *New York.* Supreme Court rules that the federal government may regulate the size, weight, and shape limits for tractor-trailer trucks that travel on national highways.

1988 *South Carolina* v. *Baker.* Supreme Court holds that Congress has the right to tax the earnings of individuals from interest payments on state and local bonds. These bonds had previously been tax-exempt.

GLOSSARY

amendment A change in the Constitution.

appeal To refer a case to a higher court so that it will review the decision of a lower court.

bill of attainder A law pronouncing a person guilty of a serious crime without a trial.

common law Law based not on acts passed by lawmaking bodies but rather on customs, traditions, and court decisions.

concurrent powers The powers of either Congress or state legislatures, each acting independently of the other, to make laws on the same subject.

concurring opinion An opinion by one or more judges that agrees with the majority opinion but offers different reasons for reaching the decision.

counsel A lawyer who may appear on behalf of a person in civil or criminal trials or other legal proceedings.

criminal case A law case involving a crime against society (such as robbery or murder) punishable by the government.

defendant The accused person, who must defend himself or herself against a formal charge. In criminal cases, this means the person officially accused of a crime.

dissenting opinion An opinion by one or more judges that disagrees with the majority opinion.

double jeopardy Putting a person on trial for a crime for which he or she has already been tried.

due process of law The legal process guaranteed under both the Fifth and the Fourteenth Amendments to protect citizens from the government's stepping in and unlawfully taking away life, liberty, or property. Included in the due process concept are the basic rights of a defendant in criminal proceedings and the established rules for fair trials.

executive branch The branch or part of the government that carries out the laws and makes sure they are obeyed.

ex post facto law A law that makes illegal an action that took place before the law was passed.

federalism The system by which the states and the federal government, each has certain special powers and shares others.

habeas corpus The right of someone who has been arrested to be brought into court and formally charged.

implied powers The powers of Congress to make certain kinds of laws, even though the power to do so is not clearly stated in the Constitution.

incorporation   The process of making Bill of Rights protections apply to the states so that people are safeguarded against state actions violating these rights.

judicial activism   A trend among courts or judges to expand their powers by making policy.

judicial branch   The part or branch of the government that interprets the laws.

judicial restraint   The belief that judges should have great respect for legislatures and executives, overruling their actions only when they are clearly unconstitutional.

judicial review   The power of the courts to review the decisions of other parts or levels of the government. A court may review the decision of a lower court and come to a different decision.

laissez-faire   The doctrine that the government should allow the marketplace to operate relatively free of government restrictions and intervention, except for those restrictions needed for maintaining peace and property rights.

legislative branch   The part or branch of the government that makes the laws.

majority opinion   The statement of a court's decision in which the majority of its members join.

plaintiff   A person who brings legal action or lawsuit to obtain a remedy for an injury to his or her rights.

police power   The power of the government to control personal freedom and property rights of people. The purpose of police power is to protect the public's health, safety, and morals or to promote public convenience or public general prosperity.

precedent   A court decision that guides future decisions.

procedural due process of law   The doctrine that the due process clauses of the Fifth and Fourteenth Amendments require that the legal processes developed over many years are carried out in a fair way.

separation of powers   The division of the government into three parts or branches—the legislative, the executive, and the judicial.

sovereignty   The highest power by which a political unit such as a state or a nation is ruled.

states' rights   Rights not conferred on the federal government or forbidden to the states according to the Tenth Amendment.

substantive due process of law   The doctrine that the due process clauses of the Fifth and Fourteenth Amendments require that laws be fair and reasonable in content.

$\mathscr{S}$UGGESTED $\mathscr{R}$EADING

Abraham, Henry J. *Freedom and the Court: Civil Rights and Liberties in the United States.* New York: Oxford University Press, 1982.

Berger, Raoul. *Federalism: The Founders' Design.* Norman, Okla.: University of Oklahoma Press, 1987.

*Bernstein, Richard B., and Jerome Agel. *Into the Third Century: The Supreme Court.* New York: Walker and Co., 1989.

The Bill of Rights and Beyond: A Resource Guide. The Commission on the Bicentennial of the United States Constitution, 1990.

*Collier, Christopher, and James Lincoln Collier. *Decision in Philadelphia: The Constitutional Convention of 1787.* New York: Ballantine Books, 1986.

Cortner, Richard C. *The Supreme Court and the Second Bill of Rights: The Fourteenth Amendment and the Nationalization of Civil Liberties.* Madison: University of Wisconsin Press, 1981.

Corwin, Edward. *The Constitution and What It Means Today.* 14th rev. ed. Harold W. Chase and Craig R. Ducat. Princeton: Princeton University Press, 1978.

———. *John Marshall and the Constitution: A Chronicle of the Supreme Court.* Yale Chronicles of America Series. New York: United States Publishers Association, 1919.

*Dershowitz, Alan. *Taking Liberties.* Chicago: Contemporary Books, 1988.

*Faber, Doris, and Harold Faber. *We the People.* New York: Charles Scribner's Sons, 1987.

*Friendly, Fred W., and Martha J. H. Elliott. *The Constitution: That Delicate Balance.* New York: Random House, 1984.

*Guggenheim, Martin, and Alan Sussman. *The Rights of Young People.* New York: American Civil Liberties Union, 1985.

Hofstadter, Richard, and Beatrice Hofstadter. *Great Issues in American History: From Reconstruction to the Present Day, 1864–1981.* New York: Random House, 1982.

Kelly, Alfred H., Winifred A. Harbison, and Herman Belz. *The American Constitution: Its Origins and Development.* New York: W.W. Norton, 1983.

*Kohn, Bernice. *The Spirit and the Letter.* New York: Viking Press, 1974.

Levy, Leonard W., Kenneth L. Karst, and Dennis J. Mahoney. *Encyclopedia of the American Constitution.* New York: Macmillan Publishing, 1986.

Levy, Leonard W., and Dennis J. Mahoney. *The Framing and Ratification of the Constitution.* New York: Macmillan Publishing Co., 1987.

McCloskey, Robert G. *The American Supreme Court.* Chicago: University of Chicago Press, 1960.

*Readers of *The Tenth Amendment* by Judith Adams will find these books particularly readable.

McPherson, James M. *Battle Cry of Freedom: The Civil War Era*. New York: Ballantine Books, 1989.

Padover, Saul K. *The Living U.S. Constitution*. 2nd rev. ed. J. W. Landynski. New York: New American Library, 1983.

*Price, Janet R., Alan H. Levine, and Eve Cary. *The Rights of Students: The Basic ACLU Guide to a Student's Rights*. New York: American Civil Liberties Union, 1988.

Smith, Page. *The Constitution: A Documentary and Narrative History*. New York: William Morrow and Co., 1978.

*Tribe, Laurence H. *God Save This Honorable Court: How the Choice of Supreme Court Justices Shapes Our History*. New York: New American Library, 1985.

$\mathscr{S}$OURCES

Abraham, Henry J. *Freedom and the Court: Civil Rights and Liberties in the United States*. New York: Oxford University Press, 1982.

American Law Reports: Federal Cases and Annotations. Vol. 77. Rochester: The Lawyers Co-operative Publishing Co., 1986.

Antieau, Chester J. *Modern Constitutional Law: The States and the Federal Government*. Vol. 2. San Francisco: Bancroft-Whitney Co., 1969.

Barron, Jerome A., and C. Thomas Dienes. *Constitutional Law: Principles and Policy, Cases and Materials*. Charlottesville, Va.: The Michie Co., 1982.

Berger, Raoul. *Federalism: The Founders' Design*. Norman, Okla.: University of Oklahoma Press, 1987.

Black, Charles L., Jr. *Perspectives in Constitutional Law*. Englewood Cliffs, N.J.: Prentice-Hall, 1970.

Collier, Christopher, and James Lincoln Collier. *Decision in Philadelphia: The Constitutional Convention of 1787*. New York: Ballantine Books, 1986.

Cortner, Richard C. *The Supreme Court and the Second Bill of Rights: The Fourteenth Amendment and the Nationalization of Civil Liberties*. Madison: University of Wisconsin Press, 1981.

Corwin, Edward. *The Constitution and What It Means Today*. 14th rev. ed. Harold W. Chase and Craig R. Ducat. Princeton: Princeton University Press, 1978.

——. *John Marshall and the Constitution: A Chronicle of the Supreme Court*. Yale Chronicles of America Series. New York: United States Publishers Assoc., 1919.

Dershowitz, Alan. *Taking Liberties*. Chicago: Contemporary Books, 1988.

Faber, Doris, and Harold Faber. *We the People*. New York: Charles Scribner's Sons, 1987.

Friendly, Fred W., and Martha J. H. Elliott. *The Constitution: That Delicate Balance.* New York: Random House, 1984.

Garraty, John A., ed. *Quarrels That Have Shaped the Constitution.* New York: Harper & Row, 1964.

Guggenheim, Martin, and Alan Sussman. *The Rights of Young People.* New York: American Civil Liberties Union, 1985.

Hofstadter, Richard. rev. ed. Beatrice Hofstadter. *Great Issues in American History: From Reconstruction to the Present Day, 1864–1981.* New York: Random House, 1982.

Howard, A. E. Dick. "Federalism at the Bicentennial." *The Journal of State Government* 62:36–45.

Kelly, Alfred H., Winifred A. Harbison, and Herman Belz. *The American Constitution: Its Origins and Development.* New York: W.W. Norton, 1983.

Kinkaid, John. "A Proposal to Strengthen Federalism." *The Journal of State Government* 62: pp.12–19.

Kohn, Bernice. *The Spirit and the Letter.* New York: Viking Press, 1974.

Levy, Leonard W., Kenneth L. Karst, and Dennis J. Mahoney. *Encyclopedia of the American Constitution.* New York: Macmillan Publishing Co., 1986.

Levy, Leonard W., and Dennis J. Mahoney. *The Framing and Ratification of the Constitution.* New York: Macmillan Publishing Co., 1987.

McCloskey, Robert G. *The American Supreme Court.* Chicago: University of Chicago Press, 1960.

McPherson, James M. *Battle Cry of Freedom: The Civil War Era.* New York: Ballantine Books, 1989.

Padover, Saul K. *The Living U.S. Constitution.* 2nd rev. ed. J. W. Landynski. New York: New American Library, 1983.

Price, Janet R., Alan H. Levine, and Eve Cary. *The Rights of Students: The Basic ACLU Guide to a Student's Rights.* New York: American Civil Liberties Union, 1988.

Smith, Page. *The Constitution: A Documentary and Narrative History.* New York: William Morrow and Co., 1978.

Swisher, Carl B. *Historic Decisions of the Supreme Court.* Huntington: Robert E. Krieger Publishing Co., 1969.

Tribe, Laurence H. *God Save This Honorable Court: How the Choice of Supreme Court Justices Shapes Our History.* New York: New American Library, 1985.

United States Supreme Court Reports. Vol. 72. Rochester: The Lawyers Co-operative Publishing Co., 1983.

Walker, David B. "Past, Present and Future." *The Journal of State Government* 62: pp.3–11.

INDEX OF CASES

Volume number: page number

$\mathcal{S}$ERIES $\mathcal{I}$NDEX

Volume number: page number

Judith Adams is an educator and writer who holds degrees from Brandeis College, the City University of New York, and Yeshiva University's Graduate School of Education. She has written a variety of books and stories for children and young adults. She lives in New York City.

Warren E. Burger was Chief Justice of the United States from 1969 to 1986. Since 1985 he has served as chairman of the Commission on the Bicentennial of the United States Constitution. He is also chancellor of the College of William and Mary, Williamsburg, Virginia; chancellor emeritus of the Smithsonian Institution; and a life trustee of the National Geographic Society. Prior to his appointment to the Supreme Court, Chief Justice Burger was Assistant Attorney General of the United States (Civil Division) and judge of the United States Court of Appeals, District of Columbia Circuit.

Philip A. Klinkner graduated from Lake Forest College in 1985 and is now finishing his Ph.D. in political science at Yale University. He is currently a Governmental Studies Fellow at the Brookings Institution in Washington, D.C. Klinkner is the author of *The First Amendment* and *The Ninth Amendment* in *The American Heritage History of the Bill of Rights*.

Author's Acknowledgments
I especially want to thank Leslie Bauman and Elsa Silverman for their encouragement and help.